THE SIMPLEST WAY
TO CHANGE THE WORLD

THE SIMPLEST WAY
TO CHANGE THE WORLD

BIBLICAL HOSPITALITY
AS A WAY OF LIFE

DUSTIN WILLIS | BRANDON CLEMENTS

MOODY PUBLISHERS
CHICAGO

All Scripture quotations, unless otherwise indicated, are taken from *The Holy Bible, English Standard Version.* Copyright © 2000, 2001 by Crossway Bibles, a division of Good News Publishers. Used by permission. All rights reserved.

Scripture quotations marked NIV are taken from the Holy Bible, New International Version®, NIV®. Copyright © 1973, 1978, 1984, 2011 by Biblica, Inc.™ Used by permission of Zondervan. All rights reserved worldwide. www.zondervan.com. The "NIV" and "New International Version" are trademarks registered in the United States Patent and Trademark Office by Biblica, Inc.™

Scripture quotations marked NASB are taken from the *New American Standard Bible®,* Copyright © 1960, 1962, 1963, 1968, 1971, 1972, 1973, 1975, 1977, 1995 by The Lockman Foundation. Used by permission. (www.Lockman.org)

Names and details of some stories have been changed to protect the privacy of individuals.

Edited by Ginger Kolbaba
Interior design: Erik M. Peterson
Cover design: Kent Bateman and Erik M. Peterson
Cover image: Landon Jacob Productions
Dustin Willis photo: Landon Jacob Photography

Library of Congress Cataloging-in-Publication Data

Names: Willis, Dustin, author.
Title: The simplest way to change the world : biblical hospitality as a way of life / Dustin Willis, Brandon Clements.
Description: Chicago : Moody Publishers, 2017. | Includes bibliographical references. | Description based on print version record and CIP data provided by publisher; resource not viewed.
Identifiers: LCCN 2016056598 (print) | LCCN 2016050198 (ebook) | ISBN 9780802495112 () | ISBN 9780802414977
Subjects: LCSH: Hospitality--Religious aspects--Christianity.
Classification: LCC BV4647.H67 (print) | LCC BV4647.H67 W54 2017 (ebook) | DDC 241/.671--dc23
LC record available at https://lccn.loc.gov/2016056598

We hope you enjoy this book from Moody Publishers. Our goal is to provide high-quality, thought-provoking books and products that connect truth to your real needs and challenges. For more information on other books and products written and produced from a biblical perspective, go to www.moodypublishers.com or write to:

Moody Publishers
820 N. LaSalle Boulevard
Chicago, IL 60610

3 5 7 9 10 8 6 4

Printed in the United States of America

DEDICATION

To our families: We are humbled to have the crews we have alongside us for this journey. You have embraced hospitality as a way of life, and we are blessed to have homes that are never empty, always loud, and continually displaying the good news.

Praise for
The Simplest Way to Change the World

Biblical hospitality is not complicated, but it is hard. It is also unfortunately absent from much of our missional conversation. We tend to drift toward a subtle idolatry of our homes, forgetting God's great hospitality toward us and undermining one of the greatest tools we have in our gospel mission. This book is immensely helpful in unpacking the astounding realities that fuel our hospitality while giving practical application for ordinary believers to engage in the radical, everyday ministry Jesus has entrusted to us.

KEVIN PECK
Author of *Designed to Lead*
Lead Pastor of The Austin Stone Community Church, Austin, TX

We're living in this bizarre polarity of unprecedented connectedness and unprecedented isolation. If you have small groups at your church, you should encourage them to use *The Simplest Way to Change the World*. Dustin and Brandon have set the table for conversation all our churches should be having.

CLAY SCROGGINS
Pastor, Northpoint Community Church, Atlanta, GA

Every moment in life, from the exhilarating to the mundane, is an opportunity to remain living on mission for the glory of God. Willis and Clements offer the body of Christ the much-needed reminder of how it's the day in and day out faithful witness of the church that changes the world. What a simple yet profound concept!

D. A. HORTON
Author of *Bound to Be Free*
Pastor of Reach Fellowship, Long Beach, CA
Chief Evangelist for the Urban Youth Workers Institute

Whether we live in an apartment or high-rise, whether we're single or married, young or old, we all have at our disposal a simple way to display who God is and how He loves: our tables. I believe hospitality is *the* way we will impact, engage, and influence our communities in the days ahead, and Dustin and Brandon have provided a helpful guide. I'm grateful for this book.

CHRISTINE HOOVER
Author of *The Church Planting Wife* and *Messy Beautiful Friendship*

Hospitality is a requirement for anyone who wants to be an elder. In this book, Dustin and Brandon unpack exactly why. But unlike a TV stunt, Jesus says, "Please try this at home, folks." In a step-by-step, easy process, this book will help you to transform your home into one of the most powerful gospel tools at heaven's disposal.

PEYTON JONES
Author of *Reaching the Unreached* and *Church Zero*
Host of Church Planter Podcast

Is hospitality the secret weapon to advance the gospel? We are all to be "given to hospitality" as it is the currency of ordinary people showing extraordinary love—which *is* the work of the gospel. Willis and Clements arm us with helpful, practical steps to fling open the doors of our homes and our hearts to engage communities.

KATHY FERGUSON LITTON
National speaker, writer, and National Consultant for Ministry to Pastor's Wives at the North American Mission Board

Dustin and Brandon refreshingly remind us that God has welcomed us home in Christ and our response must be to welcome others. Their challenge is biblical, simple, challenging, and quickly applicable: steward our homes for hospitality so others may receive His grace.

ERIC GEIGER
Vice President at LifeWay Christian Resources

CONTENTS

FOREWORD   11

SECTION 1: THE POTENTIAL

CHAPTER 1:   Small Things Can Change the World   17

CHAPTER 2:   We Know What You Are Thinking . . .   29

CHAPTER 3:   The Hospitable God   37

CHAPTER 4:   A Hospitable People   45

CHAPTER 5:   A Timely Opportunity   55

CHAPTER 6:   The End Goal of Hospital(ity)   67

SECTION 2: THE PLAN

CHAPTER 7:   Setting Yourself Up for Success   79

CHAPTER 8:   How Do You Meet Your Neighbors?   93

CHAPTER 9:   Practical Rhythms of Hospitality   103

CHAPTER 10: How Do You Get to the Gospel?   119

CHAPTER 11: Other Ways to Leverage Your Home
             for Mission   133

CHAPTER 12: Finally Home   143

APPENDIX A: SIX-WEEK SMALL GROUP GUIDE   147

APPENDIX B: RESOURCES FOR MORE HOSPITALITY
            ENCOURAGEMENT   163

NOTES   165

ACKNOWLEDGMENTS   169

FOREWORD

In the church I grew up in, "missionary" was a sacred and scary title, bestowed only upon the spiritual elite, the Navy Seals of the Christian world. We considered them heroes, sat in awe through their slideshows, and gladly donated our money to their ministries.

The more I read Scripture, though, the more I began to see, as Charles Spurgeon so prophetically put it, "*Every Christian is either a missionary or an impostor.*" The call to mission, it turns out, was inherent in the call to follow Jesus. "Follow me," Jesus said, "and I will make you fishers of men." We don't need to move to the other side of the world to fulfill God's mission in reaching the world.

We are now seeing a flood of immigrants moving into our backyards, people from remote and unreached areas of the world. We hear the voice of a culture crying out for a racial diversity that they are unable to achieve. We see the rapid rise of the "nones" in Western society—those who have no religious affiliation at all. Many people find these trends frightening, but I believe that they present tremendous opportunities for the church.

To seize these opportunities, however, we've got to equip and empower our laity again. Jesus' vision of the church that would besiege the gates of hell did not consist of a group of people gathered around *one* anointed leader, but *multiple leaders* going out in the power of the Spirit. It's a claim that very few of us take seriously: Jesus literally said that that a multiplicity of Spirit-filled leaders would be *greater* than his earthly, bodily presence (John 14:12).

Can you imagine the power of a church in which ordinary members know what it means to be filled with the Spirit of God and led by the Spirit of God? God's plan to glorify Himself in the church never consisted of platformed megapastors, cutting-edge art, or expensive buildings. The real power in the church is found the Holy Spirit moving through ordinary people as they carry His presence into the streets.

In Acts, the biggest advances of the gospel in the New Testament happened through ordinary people. Of all the miracles in Acts, thirty-nine of forty were done *outside of the church*. We need to expect that kind of ratio today, too.

The question for most of us is, *how?* How do we follow the Spirit in our everyday lives? Where are the opportunities to follow God in His mission? Dustin and Brandon have a simple and challenging answer: open your door.

The Great Commission may carry you to the ends of the world, but it starts in your apartment complex, your dorm room, or your suburban neighborhood. God has given you a perfect environment for demonstrating the gospel and advancing His mission, if only you'd open your eyes to it. It's that place you probably consider your personal and private fortress—your home. Hospitality, as you'll see here, is one of the simplest—and most exciting—ways to engage in God's mission.

Hospitality gets a bad rap in our Christian subculture. It conjures up images of dinner parties and elaborate meals and doilies (I'm not even sure what that word means—but I've heard my wife use it). Dustin and Brandon blow up that caricature and replace it with a biblical picture of hospitality, one that will fire your imagination and inspire you to act. Hospitality is a power so explosive that it truly can change the world.

J. D. GREEAR
Author and pastor of The Summit Church, Raleigh-Durham, NC

SECTION 1

THE POTENTIAL

CHAPTER 1

SMALL THINGS CAN CHANGE THE WORLD

Every Christian wants to change the world. But it's Tuesday. And so far, you've done nothing but get out of bed, make coffee, and sit at your desk for another day of drudgery. That dream job where you do nothing but incredible, extraordinarily meaningful things all day long has not become a reality. In fact, it is starting to feel like a pipe dream, like some cruel joke marketers play on idealistic college kids. You'd like to find the people peddling that idea and punch them, but you're much too busy and tired to do such a thing, because after all, it's Tuesday and you have to go to work.

After work you'll commute home, reheat leftovers for dinner, and hope that your DVR didn't mess up the recording of your favorite show. This has become your way of life—a nightly ritual of sorts, a thing to look forward to in those moments during the day when you want to throw something or take a long after-lunch nap. All you want is to be home—nestled in with your comforts, at peace with the world.

Whether you are single, married, in college, or chasing 2.5 screaming kids around—home has become a retreat for you. Your home feels like one of the only places where no one is bossing you around or telling you what to do (at least after your kids go to bed, are we right, parents?). Your front door might as well be an armed fortress, because no one who doesn't live there is getting through to disturb the little bit of peace and quiet you've found.

There's *work you*, there's *hobby you*, there's *friend you*, and then there's *home you*. And you'd love for the world to understand that they shouldn't mess with *home you*.

Your home, as much as possible, has morphed into exactly what you think it should be: a refuge from the rat race called life, which you never realized would be so crazy. A retreat, a place to zone out and unplug. After all, don't you deserve that? Don't you deserve a little mind-numbing television marathon and vegging after this Tuesday? It's just what the doctor ordered (assuming you are the doctor, of course).

Before you know it, years pass. The fortress called your home, your personal refuge, hasn't seen a friend walk in, much less a neighbor or a stranger, in you can't remember when. Sure, occasionally you open your home to others when you host events like the Thanksgiving get-together or the youth group movie night. But those times are more the exception than the rule.

You aren't alone. Many Christians have bought into the cultural view that our homes are our personal and private fortresses. In our combined twenty-plus years of pastoring, we have observed that the way a typical Christian thinks about their home isn't all that different from how a typical non-Christian thinks: *It's the place I eat, sleep, relax, and entertain myself—by myself.*

This has led to a divorce between the way we view our homes and the way we view our mission as Christians. We may rightly understand that we are to make disciples as a part of the Great Commission, which Jesus gave us in Matthew 28,[1] but that all feels very separate from what we do at our houses. We think of mission as something that happens outside the four walls of our homes—that, if anything, our homes are even a retreat from any Christian mission that we may be involved in (other than training our children to love Jesus, of course).

In doing so, however, we waste a powerful and God-ordained means of changing the world.

Many Christians have a growing cynicism about any possible role they could play in what God is doing to reconcile all things to Himself (see Col. 1:20). They think, *Change the world? Me? Really? I can barely get my five-year-old to brush her teeth. It's all I can do to get myself ready and out the door in the mornings. The world's problems are so big—what could I possibly do to make a difference?*

For many whose lives feel ordinary, being a part of God's mission to reverse the curse on creation and introduce those who are far from God to a real and close relationship with Him feels unattainable, impractical, and overwhelming. We've given up on the hope that *we can actually change the world*, because when would we even do so? There isn't much time left between waking up, rushing to work, eating meals, and preparing for the next day.

> The secret weapon for gospel advancement is hospitality, and you can practice it whether you live in a house, an apartment, a dorm, or a high-rise.

But what if we told you that you *could* actually change the world, right from your own home?

If you desire to join God's mission but have no clue what that looks like in a normal life, we have good news for you. You already have access to the ultimate game-changing secret weapon that will transform the entire way you think about your life as part of God's mission.

The secret weapon for gospel advancement is hospitality, and you can practice it whether you live in a house, an apartment, a dorm, or a high-rise.

It takes only your willingness to open your home and life to others. Many Christians believe that in order to be part of God's mission, they have to do something drastic. (And God may call you to that. By the way, if He does, say yes.) But the reality is you can be an integral part of God's mission from right where you are, without leaving the home you sleep in each night.

Why is hospitality essential? Phil Vischer, the successful creator of VeggieTales, sums it up well through his unique perspective on the need for Christians to open their ordinary lives and homes to those around them:

I am growing increasingly convinced that if every one of these kids burning with passion to write a hit Christian song or make that hit Christian movie or start that hit Christian ministry to change the world would instead focus their passion on walking with God on a daily basis, the world would change. . . . Because the world learns about God not by watching Christian movies, but by watching Christians.[2]

We love this quote because it hits a countercultural, but hard-hitting, truth: the world could use more ordinary Christians opening their ordinary lives so others can see what life in light of the gospel looks like. And what better place to watch Christians than in their homes?

It doesn't seem that hard, does it? But too often we miss opportunities to practice hospitality.

If you were to break your life into very rough thirds, you could say that you'll spend about a third of your life sleeping, somewhere close to a third working (or going to school), and the other precious third doing whatever you choose. For many of us, a great deal of that last third winds up being spent in our homes—eating, relaxing, enjoying hobbies, and entertaining ourselves. So if you divorce God's mission from your home and see your home essentially as a refuge *from* mission, you've just knocked out two-thirds of your life from any kind of missional possibility.

Brandon and I (Dustin) had the privilege of starting and pastoring a church together for almost seven years, and during that time we witnessed Christians build a culture of mission where hospitality served as one of the primary pillars. We saw firsthand that no matter who it is—from the college student to the young family to the empty nesters approaching retirement—joining God's mission can be as straightforward as opening your door and inviting others inside.

ORDINARY DOES *NOT* EQUAL INSIGNIFICANT

I (Brandon) don't remember what day it was, but I think it was a Thursday. A meaningless-feeling Thursday.

I walked out of my house to grab the mail from the mailbox, and

I saw a neighbor in his thirties I hadn't met yet who was walking his dog. I was tempted to do what I—and so many others—normally do: quickly wave or nod, or somehow acknowledge that I saw him crossing my path, but make it quick enough that we both could go about our business without distraction.

I've done that move many times. But on this Thursday a "nudge" prompted me to try something different. I changed course and walked directly toward the neighbor. "Hey!" I said, smiling. "I don't think I've met you yet. What's your name?"

He told me his name, Stuart, and we struck up a brief conversation. You know, the normal stuff. "How long have you lived here? Do you have kids? Is that your dog that's always loose and roaming the neighborhood?"

I knew what was coming: "What do you do for a living?" Stuart asked.

I hesitated. I could have blurted out, "I'm a pastor," but that answer tends to shut down conversation. I've learned that when I meet people I try to delay letting them know that information (it typically helps to build my reputation as a normal human before dropping that bomb). But as he waited for my response, I decided to go ahead and 'fess up. He nodded and then his dog dragged him away from our chat. I didn't think much of it, other than that he'd be a good person to continue building a relationship with and that he was someone my wife and I should have in our home to share a meal.

The next time I saw Stuart in our neighborhood, I noticed he had a serious look on his face.

"I have a question for you," he told me. "When you came out of your house that day and beelined toward me, why did you decide to talk to me? No one does that."

I was taken aback by his question. "We're new to the neighborhood and I'm just trying to meet our neighbors."

"Oh, okay," he said. "It was just weird, especially with you being a pastor and all. I was having a bad day and I was grumpy, but then you came up and we had this really good conversation." He went on to tell me about some relationship trouble he was having, and how his therapist had recently asked him if he thought getting involved in a faith community might help him with some of his issues. "I don't know what I believe about God and I don't know anything about Mary or Martha or Lucas or any of those characters, but it was just really weird. I thought maybe God sent you to talk to me that day."

I smiled. "Well, I don't know Stuart, I was just trying to meet you. But I do believe God works that way, so maybe He did."

I left that conversation with Stuart that day encouraged at what depth of relationship God had opened so quickly. (That doesn't happen every day, trust me!) But I also was disturbed by this thought: *how many relationships and opportunities right here at my home have I missed out on because I just smiled and waved?*

No matter who we are, walking to our mailbox from our house or apartment feels like the most ordinary, insignificant thing we could possibly do. Nothing that could happen on a trip to the mailbox could be part of what God's doing to change the world, right?

That logic gets applied to all the routine parts of our lives. We spend most of our ordinary days with our level of intentionality hovering around zero. The majority of our existence (especially the great percentage we spend in our homes) just feels so very . . . ordinary. We cook, we clean, we rest, we walk to the mailbox with tunnel vision. And quietly, unknowingly, we come to believe that if something is ordinary, it must be insignificant. We think,

- *How could my house be part of anything meaningful? It's just where I eat, sleep, and relax.*
- *How could a simple meal have any lasting value? I eat three of them a day, after all.*
- *How could the ordinary parts of my life be significant in any way? They feel so small.*

I (Dustin) have been amazed by how the simple act of rolling my grill to my front yard (not the backyard) and grilling burgers has effectively allowed me to meet neighbors, hear their stories, share our lives, and point to truth. I've never printed flyers or sent out mailers.

I've simply heated the charcoal and watched people show up. One of the most ordinary things we do every day is eat a meal at our homes. We do this small act with intentionality and usually with other people, and we simply watch the Holy Spirit bring about the significance.

Too many of us mistakenly think that in order for something to be significant, it has to be big, different, drastic, or extraordinary. It has to be something that doesn't happen on a Thursday, because Thursday is just Thursday. Nothing could be meaningful about an ordinary day in our ordinary life . . .

Those deeply held beliefs, however, quickly fall apart when viewed through the lens of God's kingdom. Consider author Skye Jethani's argument:

> We've fallen into the conventional thinking that a big mission demands big tactics, but we forget that in the economy of God's kingdom, big does not beget big. It's precisely the opposite. The overwhelming message of Jesus' life and teaching is that small begets big. Consider, God's plan to redeem creation (big) is achieved through his incarnation as an impoverished baby (small). Jesus feeds thousands on a hillside (big) with just a few fish and loaves (small). Christ seeks to make disciples of all nations (big) and he starts with a handful of fishermen (small). Even Goliath (big) is defeated by David with a few stones (small).
>
> This pattern is also repeated in Jesus' parables about the nature of his kingdom. He said, "The kingdom of heaven is like a grain of mustard seed that a man took and sowed in his field. It is the smallest of all seeds, but when it has grown it is larger than all the garden plants and becomes a tree, so that the birds of the air come and make nests in its branches."
>
> All of this affirms the counter-intuitive nature of God's kingdom.[3]

Jesus said that in His kingdom, the "smallest of all seeds" will leave a lasting impact much larger than expected (see Matt. 13:31–32). In the same way, the "smallest" things in our lives—ordinary days and meals and homes—can have a much larger impact than you'd ever imagine when harnessed with gospel intentionality.

If we are ever going to join *all* our lives to God's mission to change the world, we need to reclaim *all* of our ordinary pieces as a part of that gospel mission. We will have to reject the notion that something has to be big or unusual to be significant. We will have to view the ordinariness of our lives as significant and allow God to use our homes as a seed to be planted and grown, not something to be discarded or devalued.

If ordinary doesn't equal insignificant, then even a walk to the mailbox or grilling burgers matters. Everything about your everyday, ordinary, small-feeling life matters.

Your meals matter.

Your hobbies matter.

Your work matters.

Your home . . . it matters.

A WEAPON FOR THE GOSPEL

Thinking about our homes in this way is a wonderfully freeing concept. As it turns out, we have a more fulfilling and rewarding purpose for our homes than using them exclusively for our benefit and comfort. Instead of thinking of them only as a personal refuge, they can be opened as spiritual hospitals for the hurting around us. Instead of being an oasis of self-interest, they can be transformed into a weapon for the gospel—a four-walled tool to wield in God's cosmic battle against evil and sin. As we do this, we become the type of counterculture that puts God's generosity on display.

My (Dustin's) friend Landon, who is a local photographer, actually moved into a new home with the purpose of being a missionary to his neighborhood. (Fun fact: Landon's home is pictured on the cover of this book.) Part of his goal was to build relationships with other neighbors and to start a crime-watch Facebook group for the neighborhood. This was so successful—along with his and his wife's efforts at hosting others in their home—that they actually became known as the go-to people when anyone had a problem. We joked that he was the neighborhood's unofficial pastor. That joke came to light clearly when a few years ago someone was killed in a tragic accident in that neighborhood, and in such a devastating moment, the community rallied to have a memorial service for the man. Guess who they asked to lead the memorial? Their unofficial neighborhood pastor, Landon.

Another night, while Landon was walking through the neighborhood after dark, he noticed that a teenage boy was breaking into a vacant house. When he saw how young the boy was, instead of calling the police, he approached the boy to talk to him about what he was doing.

After confronting him, Landon walked him home instead of turning him in. When he got to his house and talked to his mother, he learned that she was a single mom and some of the older kids had become a negative influence on her son. So Landon, led by the Holy Spirit's prompting, said, "I would love to hang out with your son and try to be a good influence for him. He can come to my house any time he wants." Through tears, the mother graciously accepted his offer.

The story gets better, but let's pause to think about something. If someone views their home exclusively as a refuge for their own comfort and relaxation, there is no way their response to finding a neighborhood kid breaking into a house would be the same as Landon's response. To think like that, you need an altogether different view of your home as primarily a weapon for the gospel before it is anything else. Standard cultural values will never cause you to invite a thief into your home, but the Holy Spirit very well may do just that.

Over time, Landon built a relationship with the boy, TJ, and eventually he met other neighborhood kids who were TJ's friends. Landon started playing kickball with them on Sunday afternoons. Then he got his small group from church involved and every week they all played kickball and loved these kids who, in many cases, were fatherless. After kickball each week Landon and his wife, Jordan, invited the kids to their house to eat ice cream or cake and spend quality time asking about their lives.

About a year after he met them, Landon and Jordan borrowed a van to pick up all the kids and take them to his church's student ministry. Not long after that, they all attended a youth camp where Landon led four of the neighborhood boys (including TJ) to put their faith in Christ.

> Biblical hospitality chooses to engage rather than unplug, open rather than close, initiate rather than sit idly.

Landon's example is one of the most beautiful ways to use our homes as a weapon for the gospel. And Landon is still pouring into those kids to this day.

At that same camp, one day TJ walked up to Landon and said, "Do you remember the first time we met?" Landon responded that yes, he did indeed remember. Then TJ pointed at a group of ten kids from the neighborhood who were also there and said, "I'm really glad I met you that night. None of this would have happened if we wouldn't have met."

That story, as good as it is, may feel unrelatable to you. You may not live next to disadvantaged youth liable to break into vacant homes. But then again, if you don't know your neighbors, how would you know if you do or not? The point remains the same, however: things similar to that do not happen if we view our homes solely as a refuge for ourselves. If that was the case for Landon, then that night when he was out walking late, he would have called the police to report his boy's crime and that would have been the end of the story.

BIBLICAL HOSPITALITY IS . . .

Landon listened to the Holy Spirit's nudge and opened his home and life to the possibility of TJ experiencing Christ's love and forgiveness. That's biblical hospitality in the truest sense. Biblical hospitality is the polar opposite of cultural trends to separate and isolate. It rejects the notion that life is best spent fulfilling our own self-centered desires, cordoned off from others in the private fortresses we call homes. Biblical hospitality chooses to engage rather than unplug, open rather than close, initiate rather than sit idly.

At its core, the practice of biblical hospitality is obeying the command in Romans 15:7 to "welcome one another as Christ has welcomed you." It's receiving others into our lives—into relationship and, yes, even into our homes. It welcomes Christians as a way to walk in the truth that we've been made family through the gospel, and it welcomes non-Christians in an attempt to model and extend the gracious invitation we've received from God in Christ. Leveraging our personal refuges for this mission of welcoming others may feel like a great cost (more on that in the next chapter), but it is a cost that is repaid with an abundance of superior joys. Loneliness is traded for community, comfort is surrendered for an eternal purpose, and detached apathy is left behind for a mission meaningful enough to give your life to.

If we walk in this biblical hospitality and view our homes foremost as a gospel weapon, offering our homes for the Holy Spirit to use as He sees fit, then there's no telling what could happen. It may not transpire fast and it may not be some glamorous story that goes into a book, but God will do what He promised: He will build His church and draw people to Himself through our ordinary faithfulness to leverage our homes for His mission. It's just that simple.

QUESTIONS TO CONSIDER

- How do you view your home? Are you more prone to see it as a place of retreat or as a weapon for the gospel? Why do you think that is?

- Why do most of us assume that ordinary steps of obedience are insignificant? What biblical evidence do we have that this is simply not true? And if it isn't true, in what ways could you begin this week to see your ordinariness as something worthwhile to God and His kingdom?

- Why did you decide to read a book on hospitality? What assumptions about hospitality did you bring with you as you began this book? What do you hope to gain as you continue reading?

CHAPTER 2

WE KNOW WHAT
YOU ARE THINKING . . .

In 2005 the late novelist David Foster Wallace gave an iconic commencement speech to the graduating class of Kenyon College. Often referred to as "This Is Water," his speech is about the difficulty of staying attuned to others in the day in and day out drudgery of normal adult life, and he opened the speech with the following illustration:

> There are these two young fish swimming along and they happen to meet an older fish swimming the other way, who nods at them and says, "Morning, boys. How's the water?" And the two young fish swim on for a bit, and then eventually one of them looks over at the other and goes, "What . . . is water?"[1]

When it comes to pursuing biblical hospitality as a way of life, we immediately happen upon a major obstacle: almost everything in our culture is set up to hinder us from pursuing it. Much like those two young fish, we are so pulled by the drudgery of our everyday lives that we fail to stay attuned to God's call on us to be missional. Our default is to swim along with the current of our culture, not giving a single thought about the water that surrounds our every move and pushes us in the opposite direction of intentional mission.

We know what you may be thinking: *No! Not my home. You can't have my home!* We get it. The invisible cultural currents shape our view of our home in ways we don't even realize. So let's take a look at some of the currents and how they hinder our efforts at practicing hospitality.

CURRENT #1: ISOLATION

Turn your television to the HGTV channel and you are likely to find one of the dozens of shows where a real estate agent helps a prospective renter or buyer find the house of their dreams.[2]

We both have spent many hours watching HGTV (and let's be honest, we'll probably spend many more). The thing about a channel like HGTV is that it can actually teach you what people believe about the homes they live in, what they value most, and how they approach the spaces they inhabit. In this way, it's an amazing tool to understand our culture and the ways we are most likely to think about our own homes, even as Christians.

> When it comes to pursuing biblical hospitality as a way of life, we immediately happen upon a major obstacle: almost everything in our culture is set up to hinder us from pursuing it.

If you've spent any time watching HGTV, consider some of the most common phrases you hear there. Words like *oasis*, *privacy*, and *retreat* come to mind.

Anytime a salesman, whether a television producer going after ratings or a real estate agent pursuing a commission, tries to sell something, they go after what they think the consumer wants. And we want our homes to isolate us from the world.

Even for those located in a bustling high-rise, we want our actual living space to be private. Our homes get us *away* from others (or at least the vast majority of others). Garages, privacy fences, building security guards, and key codes—all of those reinforce our desire for isolation. There is, of course, nothing wrong with appropriate isolation and wanting your own defined space. When taken to the extreme, however, a desire for isolation is at odds with the biblical values of community, hospitality, and neighborliness.

Think about this: what if you could see a bird's-eye view of your neighborhood—if you could see your neighborhood as God sees it? Odds are you would see lots of people who may not admit it, but who desperately long for connection and community. Yet they spend most of their rare free time cordoned off in their respective homes, doors shut and locked tight, as they scroll through social media apps or watch other people live on screens. This scratches their itch for connection and community, but leaves those desires profoundly unfulfilled. Isn't that sadly ironic?

I (Brandon) have never seen this more clearly than I did last year after my family and I moved into a new neighborhood. We invited all our closest neighbors over for dessert in order to meet them, and two of my neighbors approached each other and introduced themselves. They lived two doors down from each other. I heard one of them say to the other, "It's nice to finally meet you. It's sad that we've both been here fifteen years and we've never met."

Though we hosted the dessert get-together, I admit that meeting neighbors like that is not natural for me. I am an introvert to the nth degree. So is my wife, Kristi. We both get energy from alone time— from peace and quiet and good books and stillness (at least before we had kids). At parties (when I am forced to go), I find a quiet corner with fewer people. I identify with this isolation current, the my-home-is-my-refuge sentiment, because in many ways, for me, it is. I love my home, I love the people in it, and I love the way God uses it to refuel and refresh me.

Half of all people identify as introverts,[3] so if you are one, we realize you may be thinking, *Yeah, but I really can't practice—I don't want to practice—hospitality because I'm an introvert. It would be too draining.* Please do not read this book thinking the message is, *Force yourself to be an extrovert because of the gospel!* Please don't let your personality type be a barrier to living out a God-ordained calling that is actually tailor-made to suit your personality type. I understand that introverts get the rap that they don't like people, but that's not true. We just like people in smaller, quieter doses than our extroverted compatriots do.

I have found that inviting one person (or a couple of people) to my house where we enjoy quality time together, have good conversation, and experience a volume level that never gets too stressful is actually *totally* my speed (and completely fits the bill of hospitality!).

CURRENT #2: RELAXATION

We think a primary purpose of our homes is for them to be temples of relaxation. They are the one place that is *ours*—where we can kick back, veg out, and unwind. This may or may not be explicitly stated, but the default stance in our culture is that a home's primary purpose is to rest, relax, and recharge, so anything that seems to threaten your home's ability to be a sanctuary for you may not be a welcome prospect. We believe our homes have a unique ability to restore our sanity and help us recoup after a stressful day or week, and we'll do almost anything to protect that sense of refuge.

The first home that my wife, Renie (pronounced "Rainy"), and I (Dustin) purchased was a 1950s, small, Craftsman-style, red brick home, which needed work. By no means was this house the ideal place to practice hospitality. The floor plan was the opposite of open. And when measuring its pluses and minuses during the buying process, the last thing on my mind was to look at it through a hospitality lens. As a matter of fact, one of the positives I liked most about this house was the privacy of the backyard. Not only was it secluded, it had its own natural canopy made by God Himself—huge oak trees surrounded the yard. The idea of the backyard becoming my own personal oasis was a primary selling point for me. My grand strategy was to buy a hammock, and I already had the two trees picked out to hang it from.

This thought process seemed easy to justify because that season of life and ministry was very stressful. We were in a city where we knew hardly anyone, planting a church we were pretty sure no one was going to attend, and I was getting paid a cool $12K a year. So having a domain that would serve exclusively as a place to relax was at the top of my priorities list. Wanting to come home after a hard day and not be bothered by anyone was not something I simply wanted, it's something I felt I *deserved*. Hospitality was not even on my radar, but that hammock definitely was. Fortunately, God showed me a way to both relax and practice hospitality, which I'll tell you about in a later chapter.

Our homes *should* be places where we relax and unwind. They are a grace gift from God, meant to rejuvenate and restore our bodies and souls through rest and Sabbath. As with any desire we make too ultimate, however, if we place personal relaxation and refuge at the forefront of our home's purpose, we lose God-given opportunities to practice gospel-driven intentionality.

CURRENT #3: ENTERTAINMENT

Our desire for isolation and relaxation often fuels our addiction to entertainment. There is, of course, nothing inherently wrong with entertainment. There is nothing inherently wrong with passing time in an enjoyable way—watching Netflix, playing a game, or looking at Facebook on our iPhone. We can participate in all of these things from a place of spiritual fullness, and we can use them in redeeming ways.

Increasingly alarming studies show, however, just how much time we as a culture spend entertaining ourselves, primarily through technology and screen time. One recent Nielsen study states that the average American watches more than five hours of television a day.[4] That average is quite a lot when you remember that the average person sleeps for around eight hours and works for at least eight hours per day (and that figure only counts television, not the approximately two hours per day the participants in the same study spent with apps on smartphones or tablets).[5]

The time we spend with screens seems to be rapidly filling the little free time we have, as well as much of the time we spend in our homes. There is even a new term called "show hole," meant to describe the feeling that comes after you binge-watch a TV show.

Show hole: When you finally finish binge-watching all the episodes of a favorite TV series on Netflix/Hulu/Amazon, as the credits to the final episode roll, that empty feeling that wraps around your soul because you don't know now what to do with your life. Like a good friend just left you forever.

"I think I cried three different times during the finale and now I have a show hole where my heart used to be."[6]

This is, of course, a humorous way to describe the addictive tendencies of entertainment and the "hole" it can't quite fill in us. Ask anyone who has binge-watched a TV show and they are likely to smile knowingly at the concept described here (and we certainly would be part of that "anyone who has binge-watched a TV show").

> In many ways, your culture has you set up to fail, because the dominant values and ways of thinking about your home is at odds with how the gospel causes you to view your home.

The truth is, entertainment has taken a prominent role in our modern lives. The center of many homes is the living room, and much of the "living" done there is actually watching productions of other humans living on screens. Our devices usher us into another realm, and we gladly take them up on the offer. For the Christian it is necessary to look critically at this trend, because if screens take up too much of our time and energy, that will lead us to further isolation and we will forsake any sense of mission for our homes. (We will further discuss the relationship between technology and hospitality in chapter 5.)

CURRENT #4: BUSYNESS

The final cultural factor that hinders us from practicing biblical hospitality is busyness. Most people are so busy and frantic that they do not have a vision for how a lifestyle of sharing life with others in their homes could possibly fit into their schedules.

Our time is already filled to capacity with work, school, kids' activities, clubs, hobbies, and other commitments. We run through life at a frantic pace and then finally get home, lock the dead bolt, and isolate ourselves, hoping to gain the strength we need to face the next day.

This addiction to busyness often keeps us from enjoying life the way we were designed to enjoy it, *and* it keeps us from practicing hospitality as a way of life. We cannot haphazardly live out hospitality. We must pursue it intentionally, and frankly, it needs to be calendared. Having people in my (Dustin's) home for a meal or game night or to watch a big game tends to happen only if my wife and I put it on the calendar. I spend a lot of time traveling for work, we have two kids who love extracurricular activities, and we live in a city that is driven by busyness. Renie and I constantly deal with the tension that lives in the space between our hectic schedules and our conviction to slow down and enjoy people. We have to remind ourselves that busyness is not a medal of valor to be displayed.

A NEW WAY TO THINK

The harsh reality is that because of these factors, you won't accidentally fall or stumble into changing the world through biblical hospitality. In many ways, your culture has you set up to fail, because the dominant values and ways of thinking about your home is at odds with how the gospel causes you to view your home. The water you and I swim in is polluted with things that make hospitality difficult.

Pursuing biblical hospitality as a way of life will take a very intentional shift in your life and mentality. It will happen only by offering the entire way you view your home to God and letting Him turn it upside down in the best way possible. You'll have to learn to think of your home primarily from a Christian perspective and let that mindset uproot the ways your culture has taught you to view your home.

This will take stepping back and seeing the cultural waters you swim in. Then you will likely need to drastically reorder your rhythms and priorities. If you do nothing, you will continue to think the same way you always have and do the same things you've always done. Maybe a simple movement against the current becomes a way of life that leads to seeing lives and neighborhoods transformed. Imagine hundreds, thousands of believers swimming against the current.

Rebelling against the cultural norms and turning your home into a weapon for the gospel is not only completely possible, it's a thrilling and meaningful thing to give your life to. It may just be the simplest way to change the world.

QUESTIONS TO CONSIDER

- Which of the four cultural currents (isolation, retreat, entertainment, busyness) that work against hospitality hinders you most from using your home as a weapon for the gospel?
- What changes would need to take place for hospitality to become a way of life for you?
- Why does the mission of a Christian's life necessitate countercultural living? What happens if you consistently follow the world's values rather than God's values?

CHAPTER 3

THE HOSPITABLE GOD

I (Dustin) recently sat with a group of church leaders to discuss what's working and not working in the local church in terms of mission and reaching local communities. As I talked about biblical hospitality and the vital role it plays in mission, one pastor looked at me and said, "I just don't think it works. I'm not sure how much it really matters." To which another leader added, "Is hospitality really that big of a deal?"

I was stunned. And in case you're thinking the same thing: for the record, yes, it works, and yes, it is a big deal.

Clearly the New Testament commands believers to practice hospitality:

- Contribute to the needs of the saints and seek to show hospitality. (Rom. 12:13)
- Do not neglect to show hospitality to strangers, for thereby some have entertained angels unawares. (Heb. 13:2)
- Show hospitality to one another without grumbling. (1 Peter 4:9)

These are obviously important (as commands tend to be) and we will discuss them later, but we'd also like to zoom out and show that hospitality is a big deal to God throughout the Bible. It may seem strange to think of it this way, but the *entire* Bible is a story about God's hospitality.

In the first chapters of Genesis we see God's hospitality on display in full, creative force. He creates the heavens and the earth, and by doing so fashions the perfect home for Adam and Eve. He provides everything they need to thrive in created joy.

Pick up the story in Genesis 1:28–30 and pay attention to the repetition:

> God said to them, "Be fruitful and multiply and fill the earth and subdue it, and have dominion over the fish of the sea and over the birds of the heavens and over *every* living thing that moves on the earth." And God said, "Behold, I have given you *every* plant yielding seed that is on the face of all the earth, and *every* tree with seed in its fruit. You shall have them for food. And to *every* beast of the earth and to *every* bird of the heavens and to *everything* that creeps on the earth, *everything* that has the breath of life, I have given *every* green plant for food." (emphasis added)

The word *every* or *everything* appears repeatedly in these verses. Genesis 1 reads like the most gracious host in the world is welcoming you into His castle, and He says, "Look! It's all yours. Everything! I've made it all meticulously for you." It's like a parent who beams with delight as the children open gifts on Christmas morning.

The *entire* Bible is a story about God's hospitality.

Then in Genesis 3, Adam and Eve betrayed God by willfully rebelling against His authority, and in so doing, they neglected the gracious hospitality He offered. Yet God responded with grace by seeking them out. They did not die on the day they sinned, as God's earlier command seemed to imply (Gen. 2:16–17). Instead God sewed clothes for them to cover their nakedness and shame, and He foreshadowed how He not only would provide for them through working the ground, but promised a Redeemer to come who would crush the enemy who seduced them into sin (Gen. 3:15).[1]

In this story, the biblical writer introduced a central tension that plays throughout all of Scripture: how is God going to continue to be hospitable to humanity if He is also holy and cannot dwell with evil? Even though Adam and Eve are put outside the garden of Eden because of their heinous challenge to their Creator and His holiness, God initiated a way that He could continue to be hospitable to His now-fallen creation.

In Genesis 12, God told Abraham (then called Abram) that God was going to form a special people from his descendants, a people who would be God's and put Him on display throughout the earth: "I will make of you a great nation, and I will bless you and make your name great, so that you will be a blessing" (v. 2). Then He continued: "In you all the families of the earth shall be blessed" (v. 3). This pronouncement shows that God's purpose for picking Abraham's family to represent Him was so that He could use them to be hospitable to every other nation.

This choice of a people is ironic in many ways, because this "great nation," Israel, was known to be the smallest and most alienated of all nations—the runt of the litter, if you will. Yet God lavished His mercy and love on them for a purpose that extended far beyond them.

The entire Old Testament is the story of God's hospitality to a special people, the Israelites. He invited them into relationship with Him and taught them what community with the God of creation looks like. Even though they continually sinned and turned to false gods, just as Adam and Eve had, time and time again God pursued them, putting out the welcome mat when they finally decided to return to Him.

This story culminates in the ultimate act of hospitality: God sent His Son through the lineage of Israel to make a way once and for all for repentant men, women, and children to be reconnected to God. In Christ, God satisfied His own demand for holiness; He substituted His holiness for our wickedness and His death for ours, so that He could invite us back into relationship with Him and continue to care for us (Rom. 5:6–11).

Jesus left the comfort of His home in heaven to live a hard-working

> The Bible begins with God making a home for humanity to dwell with Him in a garden and the Bible ends with God making a home for believers to dwell with Him in a city.

carpenter's life, become a traveling, homeless evangelist, and then be crucified by the very people He had come to save. And as the Son of God rose to life on the third day after His crucifixion, the door of His tomb rolled open a way for men, women, and children to finally be in right relationship with the Father whom our first parents declared independence from in the garden. God did this so that ultimately we can live with Him forever in harmony in His eternal home.

The apostle John received a vision of this coming, heavenly home:

> Then I saw a new heaven and a new earth, for the first heaven and the first earth had passed away, and the sea was no more. And I saw the holy city, new Jerusalem, coming down out of heaven from God, prepared as a bride adorned for her husband. And I heard a loud voice from the throne saying, "Behold, the dwelling place of God is with man. He will dwell with them, and they will be his people, and God himself will be with them as their God. He will wipe away every tear from their eyes, and death shall be no more, neither shall there be mourning, nor crying, nor pain anymore, for the former things have passed away." (Rev. 21:1–4)

The Bible begins with God making a home for humanity to dwell with Him in a garden and the Bible ends with God making a home for believers to dwell with Him in a city. These beautiful bookends to Scripture mean that not only did God do what He set out to do in the beginning, but somehow through all the mess of humanity, He actually made a home to share with us that is much bigger and better than the first one.

The story of creation ends with a vibrant city, coming down from the clouds in great spectacle, resting on the new heavens and new earth that God remakes out of the debris of the first one. God makes a home for us to dwell with Him, and we will be His people and He will be our God (Jer. 32:38; Ezek. 37:27; Rev. 21:3). God finished what He started in the garden, and this last grand act of hospitality is made possible only by His continual hospitality. His grace is made evident through His hospitality toward sinners like us.

Throughout the saga of history, God consistently initiates relationship. He is a gracious host, constantly welcoming in wayward sinners who deserve His wrath—a people whose only hope is that He would show them undeserved hospitality.

If ever there has been a stranger in need, someone completely excluded and hopeless, fully dependent on the grace of another—that is us. We were out in the cold, victims of our own folly, freezing to death from the coldness in our own hearts. And all throughout history, God opens the door, rescues us, and welcomes us back into relationship through sheer, inexplicable grace.

For those of us in Christ, we have been grafted into the same rescue mission. According to 2 Corinthians 5:18, God has given us "the ministry of reconciliation," proclaiming the good news that He's made a way for our sins to be forgiven, for traitors to sit at His table again. He invites us into the welcoming mission that He has proclaimed since the beginning of time.

THE GOSPEL WITH FLESH ON

Any time we practice hospitality, we put human flesh on this gospel story. The apostle Paul made this idea clear when he wrote, "Welcome one another as Christ has welcomed you, for the glory of God" (Rom. 15:7).

Welcome one another as Christ has welcomed *you*.

This hospitality applies both to other believers and those who are far from Jesus. We welcome other believers into our lives as Christ has welcomed us, and as we do so, God uses the relationships that are created to model the heart of a hospitable God and draw us closer to Him.

As we welcome other believers into our lives and homes, we create a beautiful model for what life under God looks like. We become a living, breathing demonstration of the gospel and look like salt and light as Jesus said we would (Matt. 5:13–16).

We also welcome into our lives and homes those who are far from Jesus, because this is one of the most effective ways we can put the gospel on display for them. By doing so, we physically communicate the entire story of God to them: that our sin caused the sense of estrangement and disconnection we all feel (toward God and other people), but God loves us so much that He made a way for us to return to Him.

When we invite into our homes and lives those who are far from God, essentially we say to them, *God loves you and He hasn't given up on you.* We present that message with our actions before we even get a chance to share the gospel with our words. If we are truly God's ambassadors, as Paul called us in 2 Corinthians 5:20,[2] then when we open our doors to a non-Christian, it is as if God Himself is opening His door. When Christians practice this simple action repeatedly, it changes the world.

Hospitality is not some stuffy, outdated practice. It is clearly a biblical idea of utmost importance, because it is the primary way we tell the astounding story that God hasn't given up on us. Any time we practice hospitality we follow in the steps of our lavishly hospitable God. Here's the potentially scary part: because of our role in representing God to the world, when we *don't* walk in hospitality, we do not tell the truth about God. When we are cold, separated, and distant from those around us, we communicate that God is cold, separated, and distant. When we are warm, loving, and gracious, we put the gospel on display. This type of hospitality, which testifies to the character of our God, has always been a hallmark of God's people.

QUESTIONS TO CONSIDER

- Is "hospitable" a virtue you typically use to speak about God? Why is the work of Jesus Christ a demonstration of God's hospitality?
- When Christians practice hospitality, they model the heart of God. How does this serve as the primary motivation for hospitality?
- What does your current lifestyle communicate about God's character? If you are a Christian, imagine yourself as a walking billboard for the gospel. What are you saying to the world?

CHAPTER 4

A HOSPITABLE PEOPLE

S ince the entire story of history is about God's hospitality to humanity, we have to view the people God forms to represent Himself in
light of that narrative. After all, a hospitable God will create a hospitable
people to represent Him in every age. Let's take a look at some of the
ways God has accomplished His purposes through His people.

A HOSPITABLE PEOPLE IN THE OLD TESTAMENT

From God's call to Abram (Abraham) in Genesis 12 and God's
promise that He would bless all families of the earth through Abraham's family, God never veered from that promise.[1] As God formed
the nation of Israel (Abraham's descendants), He did so with the intention that they would be a hospitable people in the specific culture
in which they found themselves.

After humanity's rebellion against God, He had to reestablish what
it meant to live under His laws and directions. First, he freed them
from the slavery they'd been forced to endure for hundreds of years
(see Ex. 1–15). Then He made them into their own nation (Israel)
under Him and gave them rules to live by (we know them as the
Ten Commandments) in order to set them apart from all peoples
of the earth who were not living under God's authority. In this way,
they showcased a compelling counterculture to the world around
them, representing what life under God was designed to look like
(see Ex. 20:1–17).

God sought to establish Israel as "a kingdom of priests" as Exodus

19 tells us. They would become God's representatives, a go-between or ambassador between God and the peoples scattered over the far reaches of the earth:

> "'Now therefore, if you will indeed obey my voice and keep my covenant, you shall be my treasured possession among all peoples, for all the earth is mine; and you shall be to me a kingdom of priests and a holy nation.' These are the words that you shall speak to the people of Israel." (Ex. 19:5–6)

It's worth noting that even in Moses's encounters with Pharaoh in the book of Exodus, one of the reasons that Pharaoh's heart grew so hardened was so God could display His power and might, both to Pharaoh (Ex. 7:17) and also to the rest of the world (Ex. 9:16). In the Old Testament's greatest story of freedom, God was concerned not only with the good of His people but also that all peoples of the earth would know Him as God.

God's intention was never to exclude those who were not already part of His people; God's design was always to welcome outsiders into His family:

> Let not the foreigner who has joined himself to the LORD say, "The LORD will surely separate me from his people" . . . For thus says the LORD: "the foreigners who join themselves to the LORD, to minister to him, to love the name of the LORD, and to be his servants, everyone who keeps the Sabbath and does not profane it, and holds fast my covenant—these I will bring to my holy mountain, and make them joyful in my house of prayer; their burnt offerings and their sacrifices will be accepted on my altar; for my house shall be called a house of prayer for all peoples." The Lord GOD, who gathers the outcasts of Israel, declares, "I will gather yet others to him besides those already gathered." (Isa. 56:3, 6–8)

Throughout the Old Testament Israel represented God and His hospitality to the surrounding nations by becoming a community that could put God on display, and by repenting of their sins when they chose to rebel against God's authority. They put God's hospitality on display when they left the edges of their harvests for the poor and sojourner (Lev. 23:22). And over and over again God showed His concern for how they treated outsiders. Consider this command: "The foreigner residing among you must be treated as your native-born. Love them as yourself, for you were foreigners in Egypt. I am the LORD your God" (Lev. 19:34 NIV).

God actually instructed the Israelites to be hospitable to others by reminding them that they once were foreigners and outsiders in Egypt. He commanded them to show the same hospitality that they needed and desired when they were in Egypt as a beautiful foreshadowing of the gospel. Through God's leadership the Israelites became a hospitable people in the culture and time where God put them.

A HOSPITABLE PEOPLE IN THE NEW TESTAMENT

When Jesus came to earth, He reinforced the idea that God stated in Isaiah 56—that His plan was not only to save the people of Israel, but to open the door of salvation for all people. Jesus alluded to this in John 10:16 when He said, "I have other sheep that are not of this fold. I must bring them also, and they will listen to my voice." Paul also eloquently described God's heart for non-Israelites:

Remember that at one time you Gentiles in the flesh, called "the uncircumcision" by what is called the circumcision, which is made in the flesh by hands—remember that you were at that time separated from Christ, alienated from the commonwealth of Israel and strangers to the covenants of promise, having no hope and without God in the world. But now in Christ Jesus you who once were far off have been brought near by the blood of Christ. (Eph. 2:11–13)

These verses drive home the fact that God's redemptive plan was never exclusive, but always inclusive. His goal was always to adopt people from all tribes of the earth into His family (Gen. 12:3; Rev. 7:9). Paul went on to establish the implications of these truths:

> He came and preached peace to you who were far off and peace to those who were near. For through him we both have access in one Spirit to the Father. So then you are no longer strangers and aliens, but you are fellow citizens with the saints and members of the household of God, built on the foundation of the apostles and prophets, Christ Jesus himself being the cornerstone, in whom the whole structure, being joined together, grows into a holy temple in the Lord. In him you also are being built together into a dwelling place for God by the Spirit. (Eph. 2:17–22)

The mystery that Gentiles are "fellow heirs" (Eph. 3:6) in the gospel produced a massive upheaval in the first-century religious world—both for Jewish people who thought they alone would be saved and for Gentiles who assumed God wanted nothing to do with them. This mystery served as proof that God's hospitality knows no bounds, that He is truly after every tribe of the earth.

As a result, Jesus sent the Holy Spirit to inhabit those who believe in Him—both Jews *and* Gentiles. The dividing walls that used to separate them were high, but they were broken down completely through the cross. In the book of Acts, this group of people who followed Jesus received a new name: "Christians" (Acts 11:26). This name, under the banner of Christ, served to unify the old identities that had once divided.

Through the rest of the New Testament, this group functions as a hospitable people in a specific culture by pursuing unity through Christ in spite of deep cultural divisions. Jews and Gentiles had never mixed, but now in light of the gospel, they had something that unified them and that ran much deeper than their cultural differences. Justin Martyr, a second-century church father, described this new Christian community formed between Jews and Gentiles in this way: "We who formerly hated and murdered one another . . . now live together and share the same table. Now we pray for our enemies and try to win those who hate us."[2]

Coming together as a people under Christ with a new name was a beautiful, countercultural (though sometimes messy) way to display God's grace and hospitality in a culture and time where dividing lines were sharp.

THE CHURCH THAT LEFT THE BUILDING

The first church, founded after the Holy Spirit arrived at Pentecost in Acts 1, was marked by pervasive love and care for one another. Unlike many modern churches, which are centered around a physical building, they seemed to be a people who lived hospitality everywhere they went. Consider this well-known passage from Acts 2:

> They devoted themselves to the apostles' teaching and the fellowship, to the breaking of bread and the prayers. And awe came upon every soul, and many wonders and signs were being done through the apostles. And all who believed were together and had all things in common. And they were selling their possessions and belongings and distributing the proceeds to all, as any had need. And day by day, attending the temple together and breaking bread in their homes, they received their food with glad and generous hearts, praising God and having favor with all the people. And the Lord added to their number day by day those who were being saved. (Acts 2:42–47)

Many Christians often cite these verses as a shining example of the health of the New Testament church, and one thing that stands out repeatedly is that these believers' faith had a profound impact on what they did in their homes. Yes, verse 46 says they met together corporately in the temple, but the same verse and the surrounding context make it clear that the church also grew in the homes of ordinary believers. They broke bread and shared meals together. They devoted themselves to prayer and fellowship with one another. They were together so often and woven together so intricately that they began to notice one another's needs and sell their own possessions to meet them.

What was the result? Awe came upon every soul, wonders and signs occurred, the community ate with gladness, and God added new believers to their number daily. In other words, the early church certainly gathered corporately at the temple, but the existence of the early church went far beyond the temple. The church left the building, quite literally, and became the church in one another's homes, around meals and prayers and shared relationships. God used this community and hospitality to bring many more to His table and into His family. Their everyday, ordinary lives devoted to biblical community and hospitality were a vital part of the church's missionary advance.

As they shared meals together and practiced hospitality with one another in their homes, they became a compelling demonstration of the good news that could create such a community. Everyone was invited into this community centered on God's hospitality to sinners.

A HOSPITABLE PEOPLE BETWEEN THEN AND NOW

There are a multitude of ways hospitality has worked itself out in specific cultures throughout church history. Christians have taken in the sick during plagues, even when it meant almost certain death for themselves.[3] Christians have used their homes as churches in cultures of persecution (as many do across the world even to this day). Christians have adopted orphans into their families, welcomed strangers and sojourners into their homes, and offered to hide refugees from oppressive regimes—whether by the Underground Railroad or in Nazi Germany.

A HOSPITABLE PEOPLE TODAY

Christians have used their homes as a means to advance the gospel throughout the history of the church, both in ordinary and extraordinary ways. In view of the more noteworthy or radical examples, however, it's important not to lose sight of the fact that much of the gospel's spread through history and geography has been on the back of the more ordinary sharing of lives through biblical hospitality—through the simple, everyday actions of Christians who opened their lives to those around them to physically communicate God's love and pursuit.

> The people around us may not be dying of a physical plague, but they certainly suffer from a spiritual one.

Hospitality is a theology of recognition, where, through simple acts, we convey the truth that wayward sinners are made in the image of God, where we say to those who might doubt their worth or purpose, "I see you! You are welcome here . . . pull up a chair."[4]

This may not feel quite as glamorous as hiding a refugee in your basement, but it is equally important. When you stop to think about how many everyday conversations and meals shared in homes it must have taken for the gospel to reach *you* from where it started across the globe two thousand years ago, it is astonishing.

Unlike throughout history, we do not suffer from a plague in which thousands of people are dying, and if there were, we have hospitals to send them to. There likely won't be a family from another region traveling through your neighborhood tonight looking for a place to stay—we have hotels for that. There aren't people in our country being hunted down by an oppressive government whom we can hide in our basements.

Although some immediate needs that Christian hospitality was able to meet throughout history may have changed in some ways, we must not assume the need for Christian hospitality has vanished. That is a great lie, which has kept us from using our homes as weapons in the spiritual war raging around us. The people around us may not be dying of a physical plague, but they certainly suffer from a spiritual one. They may not need a place to sleep tonight, but they certainly need somewhere they can belong, somewhere they can learn about God's remedy to their hopelessness and loneliness. They might be able to provide their own food for dinner, but they really need a person who follows Jesus to invite them to their home for dinner in a small act that communicates, *I see you, and if I see you, then God sees you.*

No matter what situation or culture you find yourself in, God is still moving through His people's hospitable actions and attitudes. He has entrusted you with this great thread of history to continue His mission of seeking and welcoming those who are far from Him— and that might be as simple as reserving one night a week for the sake of hospitality.

A HOSPITABLE PERSON: YOU

For years my wife, Kristi, and I (Brandon) had a desire to become more hospitable. We heard the sermons about its benefits and how hospitality represents God and we nodded in agreement, completely sold on the idea. But we always seemed to be in crazy seasons. Difficult work schedules took up multiple weeknights, then grad school classes to attend on top of work, then pregnancy, then getting used to having a kid. Something always functioned as a barrier to actually keep us from practicing the thing we knew we wanted to do, and the *this is just a crazy season* mentality never went away.

So for years it didn't happen. At least not much. Sure we'd invite a friend over occasionally, but that was about it. Then one day, feeling convicted to change and finally having the faith to do something about it, we said, "You know what? We're busy and that's probably not going to change. We feel like we can't really open up our home every night, but we do have Tuesday nights open. What if we block off Tuesday nights for this one purpose?" That simple decision was a game changer for us.

Tuesday nights became what we call Neighbor Night (or sometimes Taco Tuesday). We plan a meal that feeds more people than are in our family (typically something easy like tacos, pasta, or some slow cooker dish). We make a list of people with whom we want to build relationship—some are non-Christians we're praying for, some are Christians who are struggling, and some are people who have been on our minds recently. We invite them over. There's nothing special about our Neighbor Nights—we just hang out, eat together, try to ask good questions, and listen well.

One of the first people we invited was a friend named Kay. She'd had some bad experiences with the church, and yet somehow despite those many barriers to Christ, she hesitantly accepted our offer to come for dinner.

We have a saying in our church: "When in doubt, be there." During those early dinners with Kay, we learned just how important that phrase can be, because we had no idea what to say to a lot of the devastating things she shared with us. We had no neat and tidy answers, only food and relationship and confident assurances that Jesus loved her and we did too. Over the years we have shared many special conversations—and a lot of tears—with her over many meals together.

For five years now, we've continued our friendship with Kay, and over the years we've seen God at work in her life. In fact, just this morning, I was sitting on her porch, marveling at how far God has brought her from where she was when we first met. Although she is still resistant to church, she now has a relationship with Jesus. She has embraced God's hospitality to her through Christ, and she prays fervently and speaks of the Trinity as if God is her constant companion and not just antiquated figures in an old book. I'm grateful that one small part of the way God worked in her life was through those Tuesday nights together.

Our Neighbor Nights have sputtered at times but they remain intact to this day. Yes, there are Tuesdays when we can't host because of some other demand, but we try to protect those nights as much as possible. Sometimes when one of us gets sick, we'll have to reschedule, and sometimes our kids will lose it and make the time a memorable (read: slightly terrible) experience, but all in all, it has been a wonderful and formative discipline for us. In fact, it has become addicting. We've seen how God uses simple invitations and conversations over meals, and it makes us want to leverage our home for mission even more! Because in some small way, we are part of God's grand design for His people.

What would this look like for you? Is it time that you create your own Neighbor Night during the week? Maybe now is when you say, "Yes, I am busy, but I'm going to do this." We've become convinced that the church is meant to carry this calling with passion and urgency.

We are called to be the kind of people who:

- enfold and embrace the lonely into community.
- recognize and include those who feel invisible.
- allow God to sustain us through food, and also through the relationships He designed us to walk in.
- share the truth to prodigal sons and daughters that their Father is looking for them.

And while the everyday use of our homes to welcome others may not feel like the most exciting cause in the world, we must remember that ordinary does *not* equal insignificant. We must remember that the church has progressed through two millennia on God's power at work around ordinary kitchen tables and living rooms. God has always been forming a hospitable people to put His hospitality on display, and if you are in Christ, you're now a part of God's hospitable people.

QUESTIONS TO CONSIDER

- How have your experiences with the church shaped how you view Christians? Are you more apt to think of the church as a place of love and hospitality or a place of judgment and disunity?
- How have others' care and hospitality toward you influenced your relationship with God?
- As the church becomes increasingly marginalized and known for negative stereotypes, how can a return to practicing biblical hospitality change the church's reputation in our culture?

CHAPTER 5

A TIMELY OPPORTUNITY

Because we find ourselves in a long line of people whom God is using to put His hospitality on display, it is wise to stop and ask: "What is my role in this culture? How can I most effectively put God's hospitality on display here?"

Hospitality is a timely opportunity for today's Christians in many ways, but we want to highlight two specific reasons that hospitality is so important in today's culture. One, in our increasingly frantic and disconnected society, people are longing for depth of relationship, which is exactly what hospitality provides. And two, in a culture that is growing away from a fondness and familiarity with Christianity, hospitality gives us a unique avenue to exhibit the gospel and provides a way forward for us in a changing culture.

OPPORTUNITY #1:
MEETING THE DESIRE FOR RELATIONAL DEPTH

Author Bunmi Laditan wrote a powerful essay a few years back called "I Miss the Village." In it she says that she goes throughout her everyday tasks in her "four-walled house while the world buzzes around me busy and fast." She talks of raising her child in her home, but missing something she calls "the village I never had."

You'd know me and I'd know you. I'd know your children, and you'd know mine. Not just on a surface level—favorite foods, games and such—but real, true knowledge of the soul that flickers behind their eyes. I'd trust them in your arms just as much as I'd trust them in mine. They'd respect you and heed your "no."

I miss that village of mothers that I've never had. The one we traded for homes that, despite being a stone's throw, feel miles apart from each other. The one we traded for locked front doors, blinking devices and afternoons alone on the floor playing one-on-one with our little ones.

What gives me hope is that as I look at you from across the park with your own child in tow playing in her own corner of the sandbox, I can tell from your curious glance and shy smile that you miss it, too.[1]

While her piece is addressed to mothers, she makes a poignant point about the disconnectedness that many people feel deep down. Throughout history our ways of living have adapted and changed, and there seems to be a growing realization that maybe some of those changes aren't for the best, that maybe in our overvalue of isolation and entertainment, we've actually missed out on something essential and worthwhile—deep relationships with others.

Hospitality steps into this desire for depth of relationship and offers a beautiful invitation. To those so caught up in the hectic pace of life that they may not even fully realize that they miss the village, hospitality puts on display a treasure that something deeply embedded in our souls can't help but notice. When we are included, invited, cared for, recognized, and enfolded into the warmth of relationship, something in our psyches knows that this is the type of connection we were designed for. This inner knowledge reflects the statement God made over Adam in Genesis 2:18, that it is not good for man to be alone.

In a culture where busyness is prized, where isolation is rampant, and where "blinking devices" replace genuine relationships, hospitality offers a beautiful and countercultural rebellion. As author Christine Pohl put it: "Sometimes, by the very acting out of welcome, a vision for a whole society is offered, a small evidence that transformed relationships are possible."[2]

While hospitality has always been a primary way God has advanced His mission, our culture in particular presents a remarkable context for practicing it to go viral. People who are far from Jesus need to be recognized, included, and invited into village-like relationships. Welcoming others into our homes and lives provides a powerful illustration that the type of relationships pictured in "I Miss the Village" are not only possible, they are exactly the type of relationships that mimicking our hospitable God creates among us.

The Role of Technology in Disconnection

One of the foremost areas in which the world has changed in the past few decades is in the realm of technology. The creation and expansion of the Internet is likely to go down in history books as one of the most important inventions ever, due to its impact in changing the way we communicate, work, and entertain ourselves.

Technology is not bad. It has improved our world in drastic ways and made it easier for us to communicate all over the globe. In some ways, we are more "connected" than ever before. However, one result of how quickly things have changed is that we haven't had time and space to step back and reflect on the complete effect these advances may be having on us. For example, I (Brandon) am thirty-one years old. A fact that blows me away is that when my mom was my age, no one knew about the Internet. The iPhone wouldn't exist for another fifteen years, and computers were nothing like what they are now. Netflix did not exist. DVRs were not a thing. Many inventions that today take up much of our time in our homes did not exist.

Texting was not a thing. If you said the word *app*, people would likely think you were talking about an appetizer. You could not speak into your watch and have it remind you to do something three weeks from now. Facebook was not even a twinkle in Mark Zuckerburg's eye. This leads to an important (if tongue in cheek) question: what did people *do?*

What did people do without their screens? Did they actually have to *talk* to one another? A running joke among couples I know is that a large part of their time is spent sitting together, scrolling through their phones. They're in the same room, but they might as well be in different realities. One common complaint I hear when doing premarital counseling with a couple is "he (or she) often ignores me when they have their phone out, and it makes me so mad."

Just the other day I sat next to a couple at a restaurant and they might have said ten words to each other the entire date. They just scrolled on their phones. If you happen to live in America, this probably does not surprise you in the least. Maybe you did the same thing last night, sitting in your house with your family or roommates, each of you glued to your individual screens.

One of the most time- and attention-consuming parts of our devices is social media. According to *Business Insider*, people spend 20 percent of their time on the Internet viewing social media.[3] This meteoric rise of social media tells us that people feel invisible and they want to be noticed. They feel disconnected and they want to feel included, affirmed, liked. In *The Divine Commodity*, Skye Jethani writes, "The appeal of social networking sites is the ability to simultaneously have hundreds of 'friends' without actually risking the emotional investment of a real human relationship."[4] The creation of "likes" on avenues such as Facebook, Instagram, and Twitter is one of the most brilliant marketing tools ever created, because we all want to be liked. It's mesmerizing to check our feed and see who liked our last post, and depressing when we discover that no one has. In fact, some social scientists now describe our endless use of social media as "like addiction."[5]

I (Brandon) am ashamed to say this, but I have found that even as I have important pastoral care meetings with people who are hurting, I am frequently distracted by thoughts of what I might be missing on my phone. What if something important happened in the world? What if people are commenting on one of my Facebook posts? Are people "liking" the funny caption I put on my Instagram picture?

This same issue has been a theme in my marriage, as my wife has constantly asked me to put away my phone during family time or even refrain from checking it while we have people over for dinner (I always argue that I'm looking for music to play through our Bluetooth speaker).

> One of the most countercultural things we can do is have an entire conversation with someone without checking our phone.

Though social media is a wonderful tool with many redeeming qualities, it is also a perfect breeding ground for this ability to be "connected" without really being connected in the truest sense. We can craft our images carefully and interact with the carefully crafted images of others, but oftentimes the depths of knowing others and being known are impossible to reach via these online interactions. And even though many of us are addicted to our devices, people are starving for the depth that comes from real, in-person relationships.

A study by researchers at Virginia Tech found that the quality and depth of a conversation between two people was significantly decreased by the simple act of one of them either holding a mobile device or placing it on the table between them.[6] This shows that the tools that entertain us and have connected us more than our ancestors likely thought possible can quite literally be a barrier to true connection.

Think about it this way: what if you were to share a meal with someone, and throughout the entire meal that person was intently focused on you. They asked you good questions and closely listened to your responses. They did not act like they were in a hurry or bored with your discussion. They were genuine, attentive, and although this is hard to believe, they didn't check their phone once the entire time. What would you think about that person? You'd probably want to hang out with them again.

Here's the thing: because of the fullness that Jesus has given you, you can be that person. You can be that person who doesn't need anything, who isn't looking to fill any need, because your needs are already met. You can be the person who doesn't constantly look for a distraction. You can turn off the alerts, focus your attention, and ask, "How are you, really?" and listen with complete concentration. One of the most countercultural things you can do is have an entire conversation with someone without checking your phone.

As Christians we have a perfect opportunity to think critically about how we use technology and social media and then rebel against them becoming a detriment to real-life relationships. We can be the kind of countercultural, centered people who aren't constantly distracted but are instead focused intently on others. We have a chance to pursue "the village" we all miss by placing appropriate boundaries on our devices—especially by setting them aside for meals and long conversations. Hospitality is the ultimate real-life "like," and it's infinitely more powerful than a thumbs up on social media could ever be.

OPPORTUNITY #2:
PURSUING THE WAY FORWARD IN A CHANGING CULTURE

Christians have long enjoyed cultural privilege in America, but now we find our beliefs and values moving from the center of society to the outskirts. While our society is not post-Christian as a whole, major population centers are, and more are quickly moving that direction.[7]

In light of these rapid changes we are forced to consider how Christians must respond. If society increasingly thinks unfavorably of Christians, what can we do about that? Do we just bury our heads in the sand and pretend the world doesn't exist?

Is street preaching the answer? Do we put signs with the Ten Commandments on them in our front yards? Litter our church marquis with clever one-liners about smoke and hell? Decide to take out all the offensive parts of Scripture to make it more palatable?

Do we boycott things? Hope our preferred politicians change it all? Or maybe if all else fails, do we build a Christian commune, sectioned off from the rest of the world?

When feeling threatened by the culture changing around them, many Christians assume a defensive posture—and this is the simplest way *not* to change the world. Many resort to the relational equivalent of yelling at a driver who just cut them off, or they become touchy or overly combative (all in the name of "defending the truth"). This combative, aggressive stance may feel like the best path to stand up for the things we believe in, but much of the time it fails the "speak the truth in love" test Paul gave us in Ephesians 4.[8] In this approach, there usually isn't a lot of the confident winsomeness that we notice in Jesus' life when He approached confrontations over value systems. There's typically just a lot of anger.

Some respond to these changes with despair, throwing their hands up as if they are in a hopeless cause. These people don't see a way forward for Christians that ends well, so they wipe the dust off their hands and practice the "shut the doors and wait for Jesus to return" approach. Others respond with escapism. They isolate themselves from the world around them to the extent that they have no hope of ever influencing culture. Others become apathetic and stop caring, or shrug it off and say, "When in Rome . . ."

But if we want to move in a positive way in this increasingly post-Christian culture, we need something more winsome than anger, more powerful than despair, and more hopeful than escapism. We need love and grace and truth—and we need open homes with tables full of food.

Talk Less, Eat More

When many people in our culture think about Christianity, they reach their conclusions based off of pop culture, preconceived notions, or Christians depicted as caricatures in TV shows or in other entertainment. But how might their views change if they shared a meal with a Christian this week? When faced with a genuine kindness and warmth of a real person, would they consider rethinking their previously held assumptions?

Rosaria Butterfield, former professor and author of *The Secret Thoughts of an Unlikely Convert*, described her impression of Christians (before becoming one):

The word *Jesus* stuck in my throat like an elephant tusk; no matter how hard I choked, I couldn't hack it out. Those who professed the name commanded my pity and wrath. As a university professor, I tired of students who seemed to believe that "knowing Jesus" meant knowing little else. Christians in particular were bad readers, always seizing opportunities to insert a Bible verse into a conversation with the same point as a punctuation mark: to end it rather than deepen it.

Stupid. Pointless. Menacing. That's what I thought of Christians and their god Jesus, who in paintings looked as powerful as a Breck Shampoo commercial model.[9]

She began researching the religious right and their treatment of the homosexual community and realized she'd have to read the Bible to see where they got their ideas. As part of this process, in 1997 she wrote a scathing article in her local New York newspaper about the Promise Keepers movement. To her surprise she received back a "kind and inquiring" letter from a local pastor named Ken. Here is the eventual result of that letter:

With the letter, Ken initiated two years of bringing the church to me, a heathen. Oh, I had seen my share of Bible verses on placards at Gay Pride marches. That Christians who mocked me on Gay Pride Day were happy that I and everyone I loved were going to hell was clear as blue sky. That is not what Ken did. He did not mock. He engaged. So when his letter invited me to get together for dinner, I accepted. My motives at the time were straightforward: Surely this will be good for my research.

Something else happened. Ken and his wife, Floy, and I became friends. They entered my world. They met my friends. We did book exchanges. We talked openly about sexuality and politics. They did not act as if such conversations were polluting them. They did not treat me like a blank slate. When we ate together, Ken prayed in a way I had never heard before. His prayers were intimate. Vulnerable. He repented of his sin in front of me. He thanked God for all things. Ken's God was holy and firm, yet full of mercy. And because Ken and Floy did not invite me to church, I knew it was safe to be friends. . . .

I continued reading the Bible, all the while fighting the idea that it was inspired. But the Bible got to be bigger inside me than I. It overflowed into my world. I fought against it with all my might. Then, one Sunday morning, I rose from the bed of my lesbian lover, and an hour later sat in a pew at the Syracuse Reformed Presbyterian Church. . . .

Then, one ordinary day, I came to Jesus, openhanded and naked. In this war of worldviews, Ken was there. Floy was there. The church that had been praying for me for years was there. Jesus triumphed. And I was a broken mess. Conversion was a train wreck. I did not want to lose everything that I loved. But the voice of God sang a sanguine love song in the rubble of my world. I weakly believed that if Jesus could conquer death, he could make right my world.[10]

It's hard to imagine a more beautiful example of a Christian pursuing ordinary hospitality as a way of life and seeing dramatic change come as a result. Through her writing Rosaria's story has reached thousands of people, and it all started with a "kind and inquiring" spirit and a simple dinner invitation—at a time when Rosaria's self-described mission was to tear down the very thing for which Pastor Ken stood.

> Let's do a little less talking and a little more eating, and who knows what Jesus might do.

Our culture may increasingly think that Christians are backward, regressive, or stupid—and they may not stop thinking that anytime soon. However, we have the opportunity through ordinary hospitality to cause the same kind of questioning that happened in Rosaria—to make people think, *I strongly disagree with what they believe, but I sure do like those people. In fact, I wouldn't mind hanging out with them more often.*

Most likely you are not going to change your neighbor's views on same-sex marriage or their presuppositions about Christians by talking louder or inviting them to something happening at a church building. Think about it: are we more likely to convince our neighbors to come to a church service where we symbolically drink our Savior's blood and eat His body, or to eat a burger on the patio?

In our increasingly hostile culture, the importance of hospitality cannot be overstated. And we are not suggesting that you go silent on all your beliefs and values. We've found that those conversations tend to be more effective when they happen in a clear context of grace and love over meals than in shouting matches from afar. Let's do a little less talking and a little more eating, and who knows what Jesus might do.

What if more Christians shared more regular meals with people like Rosaria? What if the white-picket-fence couple down the street was actually hurting in unseen but serious ways and you sought to care practically for them? What if the Catholic-turned-atheist coworker barbecued with you on the weekends?

These "what if" scenarios can become a way of life for you. Those who live around you have immense brokenness and need a Savior who heals. Many of them may have never had an overly positive experience with a Christian before, and you can be part of changing that. For the people we have known who have had very negative impressions of Christians, the only instances in which that has changed have always been through regular exposure to relationship with ordinary Christians who loved Jesus and them.

QUESTIONS TO CONSIDER

- Think about two of your friends who are far from God and the church. What evidence do you see that they are longing for relationships with others? How does this longing present an opportunity for you to practice biblical hospitality?

- Why is it easier to disagree with others from a distance or behind a keyboard than it is to love our actual neighbors? How might genuine, Christlike love provide a context where you might have meaningful conversations about things that matter?

- In what ways is God calling you to ask, "What if?" (*What if my neighbors are hurting? What if God put me here to talk with them? What if . . . ?*) How is God drawing your heart to invest in particular people?

CHAPTER 6

THE END GOAL
OF HOSPITAL(ITY)

Imagine that you have become convinced to try your hand at this hospitality thing. You put in the effort to invite someone to your house. You prepare and then that day, you pace around, wondering when they are going to arrive. You feel tense and anxious over trying something you are not in the habit of doing. Finally the doorbell rings and the thought that pops into your mind (along with the adrenaline rush from the ding) is, *Why am I doing this?*

It's easy to lose sight of the purpose when you are new to a practice (and even when it's a lifelong habit). And when your purpose becomes blurred, you lose the motivation to continue. The steam fizzles out and you revert back to your ordinary, missionless life.

Understanding the "why" of hospitality is essential for that not to happen. One of the most helpful ideas that will support you in that moment of uncertainty when your doorbell rings is to have a solid grasp on the end goal for hospitality. By the simple act of opening your door you are joining in on what God is doing to heal the planet and welcome prodigal sons and daughters back into His family. You are turning your home into a wartime hospital where the spiritually hurting can get the hope and care they need.

Rachel lived down the street from my (Dustin's) family when we lived in South Carolina. My wife, Renie, developed a close relationship with her, which began with a simple invitation to join us one night for dinner. Selfishly we were looking for a babysitter, but simultaneously we felt the Holy Spirit leading us to open our home to this young lady.

When we met her we had no idea what her story would teach us. We assumed she was a happy-go-lucky girl in her early twenties, but as we got to know her, we discovered she carried deep wounds from her past. She had experienced every type of abuse possible from those she should have been able to trust most. Her fun-loving façade faded as the frail bandages fell away and the scars of her past were exposed.

Renie and I spoke truth to her and prayed constantly for her, but often we just listened. We learned that one of the greatest things you can do as a follower of Jesus is ask good questions and listen. If you listen long enough, you are bound to eventually hear their stories of brokenness.

As Rachel spent more time in our home over the next months, we were able to see tears of pain and defeat turn to tears of joy and victory. At this early point in our marriage, Renie and I were oblivious to the primary point of hospitality, but it was through Rachel that God began to graciously teach us. Too often we think hospitality is about a meal, while Jesus has a much bigger plan.

Through the simple act of showing hospitality, Renie and I were afforded the incredible privilege to care for this young lady while watching God perform surgery on her heart. Not only did we watch Him bring healing, but we saw Him give her new worth, new value, new identity, new hope, new purpose, and a brand-new heart. God did for her what the prophet Ezekiel promised so long ago: "I will give you a new heart, and a new spirit I will put within you. And I will remove the heart of stone from your flesh and give you a heart of flesh" (Ezek. 36:26).

As we watched God change and heal Rachel over the course of ordinary nights and ordinary meals, the question of "Why are we doing this?" began to vanish. And we became addicted to the concept of hospitality.

PUTTING THE HOSPITAL BACK IN HOSPITALITY

The very word *hospitality* has almost lost every meaningful ounce of its significance. Just as when you say a word over and over, and it starts to feel silly and pointless and confusing, over decades, words can also change meaning or disappear from our vocabulary altogether.

Case in point: what's the first thing you think of when you hear the word *hospitality*? Martha Stewart on a magazine cover? Stuffy, formal dinner parties? The hotel and tourism industry? Be honest, did you yawn?

Is there any part of you, however small, that responds to that word with the feeling, *Yes! Now* there's *a calling I could give my life to. I have a strong, inner desire to be hospitable*?

Yeah, we didn't think so. Odds are, your first reaction is something along the lines of "meh." That's why we couldn't put the word *hospitality* in the title of this book. Because you probably wouldn't buy it and give it a chance.

> The end goal of hospitality is care and healing—we do the caring and Jesus does the healing.

Something different happens when you consider the related word, *hospital*. You are less likely to yawn and grow apathetic. You think of something that is vital, important—even urgent. It's a place of undeniable meaning where the stakes couldn't be higher, because life and death are on the line. People who work in hospitals are heroes—accepting the many physical dangers posed to us in this world and risking their health to save the day. This is why so many television shows are set in a hospital. It feels exciting and meaningful.

As you may have guessed, the words *hospital* and *hospitality* share a common etymology. But as we have shown, they evoke very different feelings. And although the idea of hospitality feels yawn-worthy to many in our culture, the Old Testament and New Testament writers didn't see it that way and repeatedly commanded believers, in every culture, to practice it:

- When a stranger sojourns with you in your land, you shall not do him wrong. You shall treat the stranger who sojourns with you as the native among you, and you shall love him as yourself, for you were strangers in the land of Egypt: I am the LORD your God. (Lev. 19:33–34)
- Contribute to the needs of the saints and seek to *show hospitality*. (Rom. 12:13, emphasis added)
- *Show hospitality* to one another without grumbling. (1 Peter 4:9, emphasis added)
- Let brotherly love continue. Do not neglect to *show hospitality* to strangers, for thereby some have entertained angels unawares. (Heb. 13:1–2, emphasis added)

These Scriptures do not mean that Jesus wants us to turn into Rachael Ray or deal with the pressures of executing the latest trending recipes. What they do communicate is that we need to put the *hospital*, or the urgency, back in *hospitality*. Grasping that hospitality is a meaningful way that we care for spiritually sick people is why we do this, and it will be the lasting power we need to make this a way of life. Because ultimately the end goal of hospitality is care and healing—we do the caring and Jesus does the healing. The best part about this is that no special degrees are required. No seminary training is necessary to be a friend who cares about the people God puts in your path. Literally every single Christian is equipped to open their life and home to show others what it looks like to be an ordinary person who loves and follows Jesus. Imagine what could be if all Christians actually began practicing this simple act known as hospitality.

The reality is that while there is astounding hurt and brokenness around the world, pain lives in your neighborhood, on your street, in the house next door as well. There are no doubt ways to care for the pain of the world from your perch, but that does not negate caring for the needs of those who live around you.

The woman down the street from you who does nothing but watch television all day because she's so depressed. The couple in the apartment above yours who you hear fighting all the time. The family across from you in the cul-de-sac who is so dysfunctional that the primary thing they are passing on to their kids is generational sin. All of these people, whether they know it or not, need a spiritual hospital and they are increasingly unlikely to walk randomly into a church to find the healing they need.

OUR LIVES AS WELL

In his first letter to the church of Thessalonica, Paul poetically delivered this simple but challenging phrase: "We loved you so much, we were delighted to share with you not only the gospel of God but *our lives as well*" (1 Thess. 2:8 NIV, emphasis added).

"Our lives as well" is a beautiful description of how the gospel moved forward in this church that Paul planted. He shared his life with these people, and they became disciples as a result.

Over the years I (Dustin) have taught on this verse many times, that when we as ordinary believers in Jesus share our lives with others, God uses us in unforeseen ways. We have taught this concept to our kids over the years as we've tried to model what it looks like to be ordinary Christians who invite others into our lives. And I'm not saying this is trouble-free. It's not easy to lay down our comforts, our time, our homes, our very lives. The easiest thing for me to do after a long day is convince myself that I am tired and I deserve nothing more than a night of isolation away from all humanity. But it *is* worth it. The gospel is worth it, and the village-like relationships that are created with neighbors and friends as a result are worth it.

One cool thing is that over time our kids, Jack and Piper, have come to embrace this value because it's been instilled in their lives from an early age. The village is not a fictional idea for them, it is real. They have not been indoctrinated by a culture of isolation. It's common that multiple times a week someone is sharing a meal with us in our home—it has become a practiced rhythm to closely and consistently share our lives with people. By grace this has become a part of who we are, and it is driven by the elementary expression we repeat often around our family: "Our lives as well."

One evening when I arrived home after work, my then-six-year-old son asked, "Who is coming over tonight?" I told him no one, and proceeded to let him know all the reasons I deserved a quiet night. With a smirk, he said confidently, "Our lives as well, Dad. Our lives as well." To which I replied, "Son, seriously." He smiled and said, "It's in the Bible, Dad. It's in the Bible." Nothing like a good Jesus juke[1] from a six-year-old, right?

But he's right. If we are going to live as God's missionary people we must learn to share more than our words, we must share our lives as well.

Yes, all people need the local church; they also need a spiritual hospital in their neighborhood. They need someone who loves Jesus and lives near them to act out the gospel for them by welcoming them and exuding the warmth that only people who have already been helped and healed by Jesus can give. They need to experience a shadow of the communion table by breaking bread over your kitchen table. They need to see an example of a normal, relatable person who loves Jesus and isn't self-righteous or judgmental. They need your very presence (and eventually your words) to communicate to them that God is not distant and cold, but gracious and welcoming just as you are.

Your home can become that spiritual hospital, and there is no better time than now to put the "hospital" back in hospitality. But for this care and healing to happen we must shift our homes from being a fortress of comfort to a hospital of refuge.

A GOSPEL COUNTERCULTURE

When we join God in His mission of hospitality, we are actually creating a counterculture here on earth. Our homes become micro previews of heaven where we put God's warmth and joy and presence on display. Imagine this: what if your house (or apartment, etc.) became known as "that house" in your neighborhood? What if your home became a little bright spot in your community, that when people walk or drive by your door, their heads turn a little and they start to wonder what's different about you, because you don't seem to think about your home the same way everyone else in the neighborhood does? This is possible for us, because we can reject the values of our culture and pursue the values God intends for His people. In so doing, we become a radical alternative to the world's way of thinking.

John Piper says it this way: "When we practice hospitality, we experience the thrill of feeling God's power conquer our fears and our stinginess and all the psychological gravity of our self-centeredness. And there are few joys, if any, greater than the joy of experiencing the liberating power of God's hospitality making us a new and radically different kind of people, who love to reflect the glory of his grace as we extend it to others in all kinds of hospitality."[2] That is exactly the type of counterculture you have the potential to create in your neighborhood.

I (Brandon) recently had a neighbor who moved to my neighborhood in South Carolina from Connecticut, and when I met him, he said, "You guys have people at your house all the time. What are you *doing*? Playing bridge or something?" (I informed him that I have no idea how to play bridge.) Our hope is that questions like that would become more normal as our homes become beacons of God's hospitality and beautiful, countercultural pictures of the gospel. Because the truth is, radically different people get noticed. When we practice biblical hospitality, we become radical in the most normal way possible.

The gospel has the power to transform us into that "new and radically different kind of people" and create beautiful, countercultural groups of Christians so moved by God's hospitality to them they can't help but be hospitable to others.

QUESTIONS TO CONSIDER

- Since you've started reading this book, have you taken a step toward practicing biblical hospitality? Why or why not? If you have, how did it go? What observations do you have?

- What happens if practicing hospitality is not accompanied by "our lives as well"? Why is it essential that we open our homes and our lives to others?
- How does your view of home change if you see it as a hospital designed for care and healing?

THE PLAN

CHAPTER 7

SETTING YOURSELF UP FOR SUCCESS

I (Brandon) want to tell you how my wife, Kristi, and I started practicing biblical hospitality. I warn you that (a) it doesn't end well, and (b) you may not believe it's true, but I promise it is.

I've always been a "go big or go home" kind of guy. After all, why tiptoe into a cold pool when you can do a cannonball and get over the discomfort quickly? Kristi and I applied this idea to the concept of hospitality several years back when a crazy situation presented itself to us.

One day I got a phone call from a church member. He had met a woman on the side of the road whose car was broken down, but the situation was more urgent because her car was also her house. This woman, Annie, and her small dog were stuck on the side of a highway, with no money to tow her car or fix it, no food, no place to stay—nothing.

I had no clue what to do, but I went to try to help. Kristi and I arranged to get her car towed to the repair shop. While we were working out the details, Annie told me that recently she had gotten so desperate, she'd found a box of frozen bacon in a Dumpster behind a restaurant, and she and her dog sat in their car and ate it.

That story got me. I pictured them, on the side of a road, chewing on frozen, rubbery pig flesh, and I had to do something. So I invited Annie and her dog to come home with me to live until she could get her life on track.

Fortunately, my wife is a champ and happily obliged. That afternoon, we moved Annie and her dog into our spare room. Then we all sat on the back deck, ate dinner together, and talked about the game plan for her staying with us.

"Do you have a job?" I asked.

"Oh, yes," she informed us. "I have a part-time job as a life coach."

I don't remember exactly what I said, but I think it was something like, "Excuse me?"

She explained that she was a certified life coach, and that people called her to get advice. They paid her through an online system.

The irony of the situation not lost on me, I kept asking questions as respectfully as possible, and trying not to laugh at the picture of someone on the other end of the phone not knowing their life coach was living in her car and eating frozen bacon.

And sure enough, she was a life coach. When she had appointments, she'd retreat to her room and give advice over the phone. Our house was so old and small that we could hear almost every word. To be honest, I was impressed. Confused, but impressed.

Another problem was with her dog. I have never been an inside-dog person, and her dog was definitely an inside dog. We had these ancient pine floors that we'd refinished, so if a dog went on the floor, you couldn't see it, and you'd slide through it with your bare feet.

We thought Annie would be with us for only a few days; it ended up being several weeks—partly because her life was in complete shambles, and partly because we didn't know how to set healthy boundaries.

Then one day she disappeared. We had no idea what to do or if we should search for her—until she called to let us know she had been arrested for some type of fraud.

Of course, she left her dog at our house. We were like, "What do we do with this thing?" At first we felt bad, figuring we needed to keep it until she got out of jail. That didn't last long, however, and a couple days after I realized she wasn't getting out anytime soon, I gave her beloved dog to someone on Craigslist who agreed to keep it until Annie was released.

Several months later we got a letter from Annie thanking us for our time and generosity, and we never saw her again. It's a wonder I ended up cowriting a book about hospitality, right? It took a while for Kristi and me to process the experience, but we eventually landed on the truth that leveraging our home for mission wouldn't always be neat and tidy—in fact, sometimes it might end with an arrest and an unwanted dog that pees on your floor. But we did learn an important lesson: when practicing hospitality, it's best to start with smaller steps.

Dustin and I don't want you to start out with the massive implosion that I did, so we have some practical ways for you to more easily practice hospitality.

ADMIT YOUR (WEAK) EXCUSES

It would have been easy to give up practicing hospitality after the Annie debacle, but God doesn't give us an "out." We still try, though, don't we? Consider some of these excuses we offer God and others for resisting our calling:

"What If They Don't Like Me?"

For some it seems that hospitality is just weird. We think, *What if the people I invite into my life don't like me? What if they don't think I'm cool? If no one invites people over these days, won't people think I'm strange if I do?* Insecurity sneaks in and causes many believers to take the safe route and just not initiate relationships.

If you remember the story about Stuart from chapter 1 (the neighbor I met at my mailbox), I (Brandon) invited him to my house not long after our first conversation, and he said, "Nah, let's meet at the neighborhood park instead." It seemed like he wasn't ready to come into my house, and maybe he thought I was bizarre for asking. In fact, after a couple of years of connecting with him, he still hasn't stepped foot in my house

The good news about hospitality is that it's not about image management—it's about sharing your real life with others.

(though he's hung out in our yard several times). That could bother me and I could start to think he doesn't like me, but I know relationships take time to build and I celebrate any type of growth. Even though he hasn't come into our house, I'm still practicing hospitality by spending time and reaching out to him.

The reality is (a) most people won't think you are weird, they'll be really grateful you invited them, and (b) even if they do think you're weird, it doesn't matter, because your approval is secured in and through Christ (see Eph.1:7–14) so you are free to be weird and practice gospel-driven hospitality. Nothing your neighbor thinks about you can ever change the way God views you, and that's important enough to drop any amount of pressure that comes from insecurity when initiating relationships. An additional factor is that if (read: when) someone does turn your invitation down, it's probably not because they think you are weird, but for some other reason that has nothing to do with you. They probably just think they are too busy, or maybe *they* are insecure about what you'd think about them. And some people just say no to everything, and even they don't know why.

"But My House Is a Wreck!"

When considering inviting someone over, too often we can get hung up with the state of our home. *Look at this place*, we think. *We can't have people over, it's a wreck!* We believe our status can somehow rise or fall based on how others view the place we live. But if the gospel is true, any pressure we feel to have a perfectly presentable house is a false pressure.

The good news about hospitality is that it's not about image management—it's about sharing your real life with others. And guess what? In real life, people live in messy houses just like yours and ours. Few people have the time or resources to keep their house magazine-cover spotless. We have full freedom to pick up what we can and invite people over anyway. We realize kids add to the messiness level as well, and they often follow behind making a mess of what you've just cleaned. But most people will understand—because they're dealing with the same thing!

In reality, you inviting others into your messy house is actually a beautiful act of vulnerability. It's letting them see that you are a busy, imperfect human who does not live in a glass house. This is actually more hope-giving than bringing them into a spic-and-span environment, because their house is probably messy too. The good news of the gospel is that our homes or meals do not have to be perfect—we are free to be real humans who have messes and burn casseroles. Sharing our real lives with our messy kitchens and temper tantrum–throwing kids will be far more relatable to others than hosting a magazine-worthy meal. Real life around real messes is far more beautiful and compelling than a photoshopped setting could ever be.

> Hospitality is not about entertaining, it's about engaging.

One of our friends suggested that the title of this section should be, "Jesus Doesn't Care about Your Messy House and Neither Do Your Neighbors and Neither Should You." That pretty much sums it up.

"I Don't Like to Entertain."

Following the theme from the last point, people tend to equate hospitality with entertaining. When people are at your house, you may feel pressure to make sure they aren't bored, as if you are a string puppet whose job is to dance and keep them smiling. Fortunately, hospitality is not about entertaining, it's about engaging. I (Dustin) love a good laugh. I think that if they are laughing, then they are having fun. This isn't all that bad, but I often feel this pressure, which tends to push me into story mode. I'm a storyteller and if I'm not careful, my desire to see people entertained can drive me to talk too much and not listen. On more than one occasion, Renie has reminded me, "You don't have to entertain them. Just be."

When you have people over, your attention should be fixed on them, but not in such a way that you feel you are being graded on your performance. Your stock is not rising or falling based on how funny or charming or cool you are. In fact, there is no pressure to be funny or charming or cool. The gospel has freed you from any semblance of performance as a Christian, so you don't win cool points through the favor of your guests.

You are freed to simply love people as you've been loved in Christ. To pay attention to them and ask good questions. To listen, take interest, be yourself, and not rush. Trust us when we say this will be far more effective and powerful than if you were to try to impress them. Hospitality is the opposite of entertaining, so feel free to reject every bit of that pressure.

"But I'll Have to Cook!"

Since hospitality is not about entertaining, it is not about showing off your cooking skills either. Feel free to use your grill, slow cooker, or anything else that makes cooking easier for you. Don't feel the pressure to impress people with what you cook—instead, seek to bless them. Do not let perfection become the enemy of "good enough."

My (Dustin's) friend Andrew is single and in his midtwenties. He cares for people well but has a history of being a careless cook. The man has burned grilled cheese sandwiches around seventy-eight times, made macaroni and cheese without actually cooking the noodles, and once almost blew up my house when he left on the gas in the grill for far too long before lighting it.

But Andrew's determination to love people through hospitality has driven him to use his home for gospel proclamation. He makes no excuses for his cooking weaknesses, and has people in his home weekly, knowing the end goal is not an incredible meal but the care that he can actually give his guests. He recently purchased a slow cooker, and to his credit, he has now figured out three dishes he can execute on point.

If all else fails, pizza and takeout are perfectly acceptable options, because hospitality is about the relationships being built over food, not about the impressiveness of the food itself.

"But We Have Kids!"

"Do you know how crazy kids are?" Yes, yes we do. We both have young children, so we feel the weight of this pressure. It can seem daunting to have others over when you feel like you're in survival mode just trying to wrangle your own kids, get them to eat dinner, and put into bed. However, thinking back to the concept of "the village" from chapter 5, this kind of thinking is exactly what keeps us isolated from one another.

My wife and I (Brandon) have three young children, and we live in a neighborhood with many other young families. Do you know what our house is like when we have a neighborhood family with two or three of their own young ones over for dinner? It's absolute chaos—but it's the best kind of chaos. After all, you don't really know someone until one of their kids is throwing a tantrum on the floor and the another one is rubbing mashed potatoes all over the table (of course, my kids would never do that . . .). The gospel frees you from finding your justification through your kids' behavior and makes it okay for them to be very imperfect, even in front of others.

This life sharing, even among the craziness kids can bring, is the only thing that will create the village-like community people long for. We view hospitality as inviting people into our real lives, so if a single person is over for dinner and it's bath time for the kiddos, guess who gets invited to be part of that nightly routine? Single people in our church family have often remarked how much of a blessing it is to get to experience those routines with a family who has kids and feel so much part of the family that bedtime stories and prayers are not off limits to them.

Another huge benefit of including your kids in hospitality (as Dustin has mentioned before) is that your kids grow up thinking this is just normal. They grow up thinking the village is just the way we do life as Christians.

"But My Home Is Small."

If you live in a smaller house or apartment, that doesn't mean you can't leverage it for mission. In many cities, space is limited and expensive, and that leads to much smaller living quarters. That may mean you can't have larger parties, but a small table or loveseat is just as effective at building relationships in small or one-on-one groups as a large table or living room would be. So don't discount the things you *do* have at your disposal, and your willingness to share what you have will speak volumes.

In addition, you can make use of public places like parks, coffee shops, and restaurants and still practice biblical hospitality, since hospitality is more about having an open, welcoming posture in life than it is only about having people in your home.

No matter what excuses we lean toward, we need to acknowledge that these are just that—excuses—and they hinder us from embracing God's purpose for hospitality. Consider the beauty that would come from turning your home into a refuge for others—a place where diverse friendships are built with people from all backgrounds and where village-like relationships take shape around meals and games and sharing ordinary life—no matter what size your living space.

MAKE IT A TEAM SPORT

Like most things, hospitality is even better when done with other Christians. For example, if you invite to dinner a non-Christian couple you've been praying for, why not also invite a few other Christians you are close to as well?

This serves several purposes:

First, it is a way to be on mission with other Christians and make mission a team sport.

Second, it provides a way for the non-Christian couple to see what interactions as Christians look like, so it puts the gospel on display in a relationship. As John 13:35 says, "By this all people will know that you are my disciples, if you have love for one another." Letting others see a picture of Christian community and the way we relate to one another through grace is an incredible gift and exhibits truth in ways they may not see otherwise. I (Dustin) have seen this time and again with one of my best friends, Vince, who is not a believer *yet*. On numerous occasions, he sees our friend Andrew, who is a believer, and me confront each other, confess sin to each other, repent, and walk in forgiveness with each other. I am unapologetically Christian in the way I live in front of Vince. He respects me more for that than if I hid it. He has commented specifically about how Andrew and I have each other's backs in a way that he has not seen before. I believe what he is seeing is a community centered on the cross, since the cross confronts our sin, causes confession, leads to repentance, and delivers forgiveness. Those ideas are the simple values that Andrew and I live out consistently in front of Vince.

Third, the people you are building relationship with may connect better with your other Christian friends. Our friend Micah and his wife, Laurie, have consistently practiced hospitality as a team with other Christian friends. Not long ago they were having a party in their front yard (yes, the front yard is a purposeful idea) when a couple walked by and stopped to check out what was cooking on the grill and who was winning the game of cornhole.

Micah had never met them, so he struck up a conversation with the guy, Mark. Standing with Micah was another believer, Andrew (yes, the same Andrew). They chatted about golf, family, their jobs, and gun ranges. It just so happened that Andrew had recently purchased a gun and wanted to go to the range. Mark and Andrew ended up going there together without Micah, who didn't even get invited. But Micah was okay with that. He was simply the conduit for a better connection for God to use to lead toward gospel conversations.

We have both noticed times when our friends have more in common with our neighbors and are hitting it off, so we step back and watch their relationship grow. No need for jealousy, since we have a common goal: connecting people with Jesus.

Fourth, in our experience, if you invite multiple people for dinner and one cancels at the last minute, you aren't sitting by yourself with a bunch of food. You still get to enjoy it with others.

Even within a nuclear family or set of roommates, you can break down responsibilities according to giftedness to make hosting people less daunting. For example, in Brandon's marriage, he is more of the relational connector, so he typically takes the lead in who is invited.

But his wife is by far a better cook and host, so she takes the lead in that for a win/win. Whereas for Dustin, he loves cooking while Renie makes a lot of the connections through relationships that she has in their neighborhood.

Whenever possible make hospitality a team sport with other believers. It will be more fun, provide accountability, and in many ways, will be even more effective.

CREATE A SYSTEM

My (Brandon's) life runs off to-do lists and calendars, because I find that when we create a practical system to help us plan hospitality it eases the burden.

Kristi and I have used multiple ways to accomplish this, but one that is particularly effective is creating a spreadsheet that functions as a planning tool. We made a shared Google spreadsheet to schedule our Neighbor Night invites. When we'd come into contact with someone we wanted to invite over at some point, we would add them to the bottom in the brainstorm section, and then every few weeks, we sat together and scheduled the invitations and then called or texted people. When we do this in conjunction with praying for the people on our list and being attentive to who God is directing our thoughts and interactions to, it can be a powerful instrument.

You can also put your smartphone to use in a number of ways to drive a lifestyle of hospitality. One simple way is to use your calendar to schedule and remind you of times you want to have people over for a meal or for any other reason. Simply put the event in your calendar and set your alerts to remind you so you can invite people and plan accordingly. You can also use reminders, journaling apps, or the "favorites" function on your contact list to pray for or check in with your neighbors.

The above ideas may not work for you—creating a spreadsheet may be essentially the same as someone scratching a blackboard. That's okay! There is no end to the creative ways you can schedule hospitality. For instance, Renie, my (Dustin's) wife, doesn't necessarily fit into the above category. While she is organized—and we have put in place systems for how and when to invite people over (and we do use our calendar app)—she thrives on spontaneity. These have been some of the most fruitful moments of hospitality for us. We have some Friday nights where at 4:00 p.m. we text a group of random friends and neighbors or maybe a new friend we met that day and say, "Bring whatever food you want and let's all eat and hang out!"

This drove me nuts for a while because I would prefer to plan the menu, know exactly who is coming, and make sure we are not all stuck eating fourteen different types of pasta salad. But the spontaneous nature of the night adds a certain fun factor to it, and people have loved it.

Whereas Brandon and Kristi's system when meeting someone new is to add them to their spreadsheet with the intentionality of having them over for a dinner or game night, Renie and I from time to time just ask people if they want to come over that very night. Either way, the primary point is not a spreadsheet, but the intentionality to initiate relationship and create a system that works for you.

SIMPLIFY THE DETAILS

When inviting people to your home, please don't feel pressured to do anything elaborate. The purpose is not to wow with the most amazing food or impress with your immaculately decorated home. In fact, if that were the purpose, it would not be hospitality you are practicing—it would be showing off.

So do whatever you need to in order to make hospitality feel less overwhelming. Simple meals are fine. Do something easy to eat and clean up, like tacos, pasta, a slow cooker dish, or something you can grill. Also, just because you are hosting doesn't mean you have to provide everything. Ask them to bring something, if that would be helpful. In fact, we've found that most people *want* to contribute something—it makes them feel better about coming. So let them.

The important thing to remember is that *the purpose for having people over is relationship—not the food.* Feel free to cook normal, not-so-special meals because the meal is just what relationship happens over. While food is wonderful, it isn't the most important thing that will happen around your table.

On the topic of clean up, many people dread that moment where everyone leaves and you're staring at the mess, wanting nothing more than not to have to clean it up. We all wish clean up was more like the clap on/clap off light. So get your guests in on the action. Many will actually offer to help clean up without your asking. Your tendency may be to say, "No, don't worry about that, we've got it." Which is fine if you really mean that and want to serve your guests by cleaning up, but we actually let others help any time they offer. For one, it makes clean up faster and easier, and for another, it's actually more fun and relationship-building to clean up together after the meal you just shared.

After all, if we're pursuing the idea of sharing life and becoming the type of village we previously described, part of that will likely include washing dishes together.

PUT HOSPITALITY IN YOUR BUDGET

In Matthew 6:21, Jesus said, "Where your treasure is, there your heart will be also." He was teaching that we can look at our budgets and quickly find what we love and care most about. It's possible for this principle to work the opposite way as well: what we leverage our money for can train our hearts to love that thing. This is the root of "investing," because when we put our money into something, we now become more interested, or invested, in that particular thing. If we buy stock in a company, our relationship to that company changes— we will love it more and want it to succeed.

We can train our hearts to love and value hospitality by putting resources toward hosting people in our homes. This doesn't have to be extravagant, and for most people, it can't be. But it may cost a little money to have people over consistently and provide food or drinks for them. Seeing this as a price of welcoming others as Christ has welcomed us will not only help us justify the cost, but also learn to love the fact that we get to leverage our resources for God's mission. Just as with any area of generosity, we learn that it is more fulfilling to share what we have with others than to spend it all on ourselves.[1]

I (Brandon) have a friend in my church named Johnathon. He recently got a raise at his job, and he decided to put that money toward being hospitable to his neighbors. Think about that. What do *you* usually do first when you get a raise? Maybe think about a new car or some other increase in your standard of living?

Johnathon planned monthly cookouts for his neighborhood and passed out flyers to everyone he could. He also invited guys from his small group and other church members who lived in his area so they would have a good base of Christian community to invite others into. This practice has been incredibly fruitful, and it would never have come about without him deciding to dedicate what resources he could to practice hospitality as a way of life.

A GOOD ADDICTION

I (Brandon) have a confession to make: I recently started doing CrossFit (a type of exercise program that features high-intensity group workouts).

I (Dustin) also have a confession: I consistently make fun of Cross-Fit, as I believe it's for people who were never successful in sports growing up (relax, CrossFit friends), and I am stunned that it took Brandon this long to force some CrossFit illustration into this book . . .

Okay, my jealous friend Dustin can quit hijacking my story and go back to eating his potato chips and dreaming of being in shape enough to make it through *one* CrossFit workout. As I (Brandon) was saying . . . for the longest time I heard about the benefits of CrossFit but had no interest in joining because of how much effort it would require. Sure, I'd probably actually get in shape instead of rotting away physically as I was doing, but I'd also have to plan my schedule around it, get less sleep, and sweat a lot. I hate sweating. All of it sounded too difficult.

Finally I made myself try it for a few weeks. And I got addicted. It's exactly the type of atmosphere and accountability I needed to get back in shape, and if you were to ask me now if it is worth all the sweat and planning and effort, I would say, "Absolutely!" because I feel physically better than I ever have.

Hospitality is a lot like that. It requires effort, planning, and sweat. But when paired with gospel intentionality, it is absolute magic, and when you watch God eradicate others' loneliness and transform lives, it becomes addicting in the best way possible.

QUESTIONS TO CONSIDER

- What excuses do you make in order to avoid practicing biblical hospitality? What truths do you need to remember in order to counter these objections?
- Who can you team up with to practice team hospitality? Obviously, if you are married, this is the place to begin. But what other neighbors or church members could you partner with as well? In what ways can this make practicing hospitality easier?
- Which practical steps in this chapter did you most connect with? In what ways can they help you practice a hospitable lifestyle? What other steps can you take to build "hospitality reminders" into your life?

CHAPTER 8

HOW DO YOU MEET YOUR NEIGHBORS?

W e are certain that at this point you're now inviting others into your home and your life for the sake of the gospel. You've even dusted off your old cookbook and tried to figure out a few easy recipes you can master. The biggest challenge isn't picking a night or a meal, however; the biggest challenge is often finding someone to invite. How will you find this person? Is he or she someone you've known for a while or someone new to you? If the person is new, how will you meet and actually invite them into your home?

Some people may have plenty of names on their list, while others may struggle to come up with even one. Whichever is true for you, there is one sure reality: we can all use help in initiating relationships with those God calls us to love.

START WITH WHO YOU KNOW

The first thing to remember on this journey is the nature of God. He is sovereign, meaning He rules over all things. He orchestrates all things for His purposes, including who lives, works, and plays near you. You may not consider these people as gifts from God because they have been part of your life for so long that they've become a backdrop. You are prone to miss them. But every day you pass people who could be blessed through your hospitality.

This Sunday as you gather with other believers at your local church, pick out a few people and ask them to have dinner at your house that evening or sometime that week. The Bible is clear in Romans 12 that we are to practice hospitality with other brothers and sisters. Let's not overcomplicate what may be a simple step of obedience—look around and invite.

Beyond your church, this category includes people you work with. You know, the ones you see every weekday but don't think much about when you leave your job? Your workplace can be an incredible breeding ground for relationships that are ripe for biblical hospitality.

My (Dustin's) friend Steve is the ultimate example of this. Through his career as a high-powered leader in a large company, he was constantly on the lookout for coworkers to invite into his life. Having worked decades at the same company, he pursued countless lunch meetings with coworkers to invest in their lives and invited many people to his home.

Think about your coworkers or those at your church. Are any of those relationships ripe for gospel-centered intentionality? Do any of them need compassionate companionship? Would it make sense to invite them out to lunch or to a party at your house or just over for coffee and to hang out? Start with who you already know and see what God does there.

TAKE WHAT IS NORMAL AND MAKE IT INTENTIONAL

Once you consider those people you already know, from there increase your vision to those you see regularly at the gym, those you meet at the coffee shop, or those who frequent the same park as your family. You don't need to add another task to your already-busy schedule. Instead, think like a missionary when living out your normal, everyday activities. Rather than seeing an area of your life as a thoughtless arena to get through like a zombie, you can infuse missional hospitality into it. In other words, start with your normal routines and use those more intentionally.

Look at the other "normal" places you go and things you do. What would it look like if you were intentional with the barista, the store manager, or your kid's soccer coach? You might consider each of these places a new mission field. In each location, you have a God-given chance to build relationships with those whom you might one day invite into your home.

And the best thing is that you haven't added anything new to your plate. You are just living life with a new perspective. In fact, you might even be able to leverage things that you really enjoy—hobbies like hunting or ultimate Frisbee—and form relationships through these venues.

When we lived in the same city, we played together in a summer Frisbee league for years. That was a great environment to have fun with others and build relationships. My wife and I (Dustin) struck up a friendship with a local doctor who happened to be incredibly athletic and loved ultimate Frisbee as much as we did. Our friendship with Dr. "D" grew beyond the Frisbee fields to some local restaurants and eventually to our house. Through a simple hobby we loved, we were able to eventually share the gospel with Dr. "D" on numerous occasions, and though she has yet to become a believer, we know we planted many seeds during our conversations with her.

FOCUS ON THOSE WHO LIVE CLOSE TO YOU

After starting with the people you already know, the next step is to meet people you don't yet know. Your geographical neighbors are a great place to start. With this challenge in particular, we have found a few specific things that prove to be very helpful in meeting your neighbors.

Be Willing to Initiate

We cannot sit and wait for others to come to us. Part of the nature of hospitality is that you are the one extending the welcome to others. You are the one putting yourself out there and risking indifference or rejection. This risk is most noticeable when you first initiate the relationship.

Picture this: You walk out of your house or apartment and you see a neighbor you don't know. What happens? Do you acknowledge that person's presence? Do you smile and quickly wave? What are the chances that they are going to come bouncing up to you and introduce themselves? (Not very high, right?) The likely outcome will be some sort of brief acknowledgment (if that) and you might never see that person again.

For that very reason, you have to be the one willing to initiate relationship. We know this is scary. It might make you feel awkward or downright nauseated, but you have to push through your insecurities and take a risk.

If you are thinking, *How do I meet them and it not be weird?* We have a simple solution for you: the Always Rule.

The Always Rule means that if you see a neighbor you don't know, pause whatever you're doing and meet them. Always. If you're walking to the car and are in a hurry, if you're getting groceries out of the car, if you're picking up a package—always. I (Brandon) needed to create this rule to help myself, because as mentioned earlier, I'm an introvert.

Do I ever break the Always Rule? Of course. (I guess that makes it the Sometimes Rule, but whatever.) It seems there is never a perfect time to meet a neighbor I don't know, and they tend to walk by at the worst moments. The point of the Always Rule is that if I don't decide beforehand and a neighbor walks by while I'm trying to get my toddler out of the car, I will almost never choose to stop and go meet them. So I *decide in advance* in order to take the decision-making question out of it.[1]

The process for doing this is extremely simple: I walk up to them, I smile, and I say: "I don't think I've met you yet. I'm Brandon. What's your name?" That's it. That's how I start every single time. (Except for the time I yelled, "The Goonies!" at a guy wearing a Goonies T-shirt, but that worked out well too). Most of the time I go on to ask a few questions—things like how long they've lived in the neighborhood, where they are from, what they do for a living, how they like living in the neighborhood, etc. If I know about a Neighbor Night my wife and I have open in the near future, sometimes I'll invite them to that. If I'm in a hurry, though, I just remember their name for the next time I see them and say, "I'll see you around!" as I rush off to the meeting I'm late to or wrangle my screaming baby.

Recently I heard a story from a member of my church, Tyrone, about how he never used to talk to his neighbors until he heard a sermon about hospitality. Soon after the sermon he was in his yard when his neighbor also walked out into his adjacent yard. Typically, Tyrone would have ignored the man, but he decided to initiate a conversation. Tyrone's wife had just baked banana bread, so Tyrone grabbed a loaf and offered it to his neighbor. The neighbor gratefully accepted and said, "Wow, banana bread. I haven't had this since my mother died." This simple act of initiation and some missional banana bread opened an amazing opportunity for relationship with his neighbor. Tyrone is still building relationship with him and praying for him.

Go Outside

This may come as a news flash, but your neighbors don't live in your house. So if you never leave your humble abode, you'll never meet any of your neighbors. They are not going to bust up in your living room and introduce themselves, and if they do you should call the cops ASAP.

This means you need to go outside. Often. Daily. Consistently. As much as you can. Because that's pretty much the only place you are going to meet people who live close to you.

Going on walks is a brilliant way to meet those in your neighborhood, and it also gives you the added benefit of exercise. If you have a dog or kids, that's another benefit, because people are often more interested in meeting your pet or children than they are you. Get out that leash or stroller and get moving, and as you see people you don't know, practice the Always Rule rather than the Sometimes Rule. As you walk, pray for the people you meet, the neighbors you already know, and even the people you don't yet know.

If you have a park, playground, or pool near your neighborhood, this is a no-brainer place for you to frequent, because it's where other neighbors gather. For us these environments have been a fruitful place to meet and build relationship with neighbors.

Another thing that helped me (Dustin) was moving our grill from the back of our house to the front. Though it seems redneck (I didn't say I put a weight bench out front), this switch has been an incredible opportunity to meet neighbors. People see me grilling in my front yard and it's almost as though they can't *not* come talk to me—they're either drawn by the incredible smell or they just have to meet this weirdo who is grilling on his front lawn. Either way, it works!

Get Creative

I (Dustin) planted and pastored a church in Columbia, South Carolina, for seven years before moving to the Atlanta area. Honestly, when my wife and I lived in South Carolina we were not great at engaging with our neighbors. We connected with some, but we struggled to link up with those who actually resided next door. I'm not sure what happened. Maybe a memo went out to the neighbors that said: "Beware: Pastor's House." All I know is that I rarely talked to my neighbors and they rarely spoke to me. Over time, we just stopped making the effort all together.

So what do we do? Build a wall and let them know how we really feel? Move? Obviously that is not the answer, but for us (through God's providence and not our own) we *did* actually end up moving, but not just down the street. We moved to a different state.

> Don't give up when things don't go the way you want them to, because they almost certainly won't.

In the midst of our move to Atlanta we were pumped because we believed that we'd immediately meet new neighbors who would bring us funfetti cupcakes on day one—because who doesn't like funfetti cupcakes?

Believe it or not, that did not happen. Not on day one or on day thirty.

Even though we didn't get cupcakes, we were able to hit the reset button with a new community, new neighborhood, new street, and new neighbors residing next door. But this did not happen overnight, and it was not magically easy. It took us being very intentional even to *meet* our neighbors. But we stuck to it.

My opportunity to hit the reset button on hospitality was through a God-ordained move to a different state, but for you it is probably not putting a For Sale sign out front. Instead it may be putting a date on the calendar and saying, "This is the day I start over." Be disciplined, intentional, and obedient to what God may be calling you to as you hit the reset button to implement or adjust your life rhythms for the sake of hospitality. And most importantly, don't give up when things don't go the way you want them to, because they almost certainly won't.

Unfortunately most of us live in a society of isolation where garage doors or doormen act as a moat around our personal fortress. Once the "gate" is closed, there is no getting in. This sounds a bit creepy, but I (Dustin) tried for a long time to meet one of our neighbors, Lee, and was unsuccessful. I finally figured out when he took out his trash every week and "by chance" I began taking out my trash at the same time.

"Hey, Lee, funny seeing you here," I said. It took time, but the conversations on our trash runs moved from greeting each other across the street to hanging out in the street catching up on the week. Even through something as simple as taking out the trash, we can get creative with our intentionality.

Here in Atlanta, I had one neighbor I swore was in witness protection because he was so reclusive. I tried everything I could think of to meet him, but nothing worked. Finally one day I sent my four-year-old and six-year-old kids to knock on the door (FYI, this is not a parenting book) and invite them to join us for a cookout in the front yard. It worked.

Effort, creativity, intentionality, and dying to self are all concepts that translate into practical actions of meeting those around us and inviting them into our homes and lives.

Use Technology

While technology can fuel isolation and individual entertainment as we discussed in chapter 5, it can also connect people. One helpful way to do this is to watch TV shows with others rather than alone.

Have neighbors over on Sunday nights who like the same show as you. Host watching parties for your local sports teams. Doing this exposes commonalities and creates shared experiences that foster deeper relationships.

Another way to use technology is to take advantage of social media avenues like Facebook. My (Dustin's) wife, Renie, had actually deleted her Facebook account because she felt it had become a black hole for her time (which it certainly can be!). But she had a strong desire to have women in our neighborhood over, and she knew many of them would like to read, so she reactivated her account and used our neighborhood Facebook group as the primary channel to invite women to the first event.

I still remember the night she launched the group—we had more than thirty women crammed into our living room. One, who had lived in the neighborhood for more than fifteen years, stated, "I haven't really met a lot of people because everyone just seems so busy." That broke my heart. Thankfully, now on a monthly basis, a couple dozen women gather in our home to discuss their latest book while eating cookies and talking about life. God is using this simple act to bond women who would otherwise not have connected, and it all started with a heart for hospitality and a Facebook group.

You can use social media and other apps in positive, redeeming ways when you approach them with the desire to engage and foster relationships. Recently Washington, D.C.–based church-planting guru Clint Clifton said, "The best church planting website is meetup.com."[2] Although meetup.com is not a Christian organization, its mission is to facilitate "neighbors getting together to learn something . . . do something . . . share something."[3] We don't need to re-create the wheel or start a Christian running group when we can simply jump on an app that is already out there and find others who run, and in due time have them all over to your home to hang out. You can leverage any social media outlet to build connections. In time, the goal is for you to transition as many relationships as possible from online to real life.

Neighborhood Facebook groups or local community-driven apps

like Nextdoor are great examples of ways to foster real-life relationships with those who live close to you. In my (Brandon's) life, one of the most helpful things I've found to drive missional relationships and hospitality is an app called GroupMe. It's one of the many group-messaging apps, where you can create a different group for any purpose and easily communicate with one another, add new members, etc. It makes communication and event planning super quick and easy.

Meeting your neighbors may not always be easy, but it is possible! Once you get into the habit of identifying those you can invite into your world, you can move on to building rhythms for making hospitality a way of life.

QUESTIONS TO CONSIDER

- Do you practice the Always Rule or is it more often the Sometimes Rule? Or is your style more the Almost Never Rule? In what ways could you initiate a conversation with someone new this week?

- What is one creative step you could take to practice biblical hospitality? It might be baking cookies for the neighbors or throwing a party to usher in the start of college football season. What would you need to do in order to make this creative idea a reality?

- How can you leverage technology to create relationships with others without using technology to foster your own isolation?

CHAPTER 9

PRACTICAL RHYTHMS OF HOSPITALITY

The goal is for hospitality to be so integrated into your life that it becomes second nature—that you would practice it without thinking, because it's just the way life works for you. In other words, it needs to progress from, "I practice hospitality on Tuesday nights but don't think about it much beyond that" to, "I am always thinking of how I can be hospitable in light of the gospel, and Tuesday nights are a small part of that."

We all have regular rhythms—you know, the facets of life that we do day in and day out. Eating meals is a regular rhythm. Working is a rhythm. Exercising is a rhythm. Being part of a church community is rhythm. In the same vein, hospitality can become a rhythm too.

For that to happen, you must assess your preexisting rhythms and see how you can leverage them for biblical hospitality. For example, you already likely eat three meals a day. Meals are something you can easily include others in and make into a weapon for the gospel. The same goes for any other existing life rhythm, which you might use to meet and invite people into your life, as we discussed in the previous chapter.

Just as we need to be intentional about meeting people, we need to be intentional about inventing new rhythms that foster hospitality. Since we seek to be hospitable people, and not merely people who practice hospitality, we need to find ways to build our lives around this goal. Sure, it will take time. But with a little thought and practice, those rhythms will become habits, and habits become a way of life.

With that in mind, let's look at rhythms you might implement on a weekly, monthly, and yearly basis. Some of these you may already do and so you can leverage them for hospitality, and some will be new ideas that you could weave into the hospitality rhythm of your life.

WEEKLY RHYTHMS

You can build rhythms into a regular week in much the same way you might have a weekly standing date night or have to take your child to soccer practice. Consider the following ideas.

Neighbor Night/Taco Tuesday

We've already discussed how starting Neighbor Night was an integral part of starting a lifestyle of hospitality for my (Brandon's) family. This is a great, practical first step to reserve one night a week (or one night every other week) and devote it specifically to hospitality. Make a plan for who you'd like to invite, invite them, have fun, and see what Jesus does.

There are many variations to this idea. You can call it Taco Tuesday (or anything else you like) and even make it an open invite to all your neighbors every week. You could make it a "bring your own meat" grilling party. Or Soup and Salad Saturdays. The important part is to make it a regular rhythm, tweaking it to be most effective for your context and not giving up if it doesn't start the way you'd like it to.

My (Dustin's) Coloradoan friend, Alan, started a similar, creative weekly gathering for his neighbors. He calls it Free Coffee Friday, and he simply provides coffee for his neighbors before they and their kids head off to work or school. He pulls out a couple of eight-foot folding tables, plastic chairs, and some decent coffee made in the old classic urns. Neighbors not only come—they love it. People gather around, serve themselves coffee, talk about the week behind them and the weekend that lies ahead.

This rhythm even includes school bus drivers who cover the neighborhood, as well as teachers and administrators from the local school. Alan's commitment to Free Coffee Friday, or just to caffeine, is real, since he's agreed to offer it rain, shine, or snow. In talking with Alan about it, he said he started with a desire to fill the crack of loneliness in the neighborhood and to create a community environment for parents to talk with their kids—and of course to caffeinate for the day. Alan said, "The coffee is mediocre, but the connections run deep by the end of the school year. Really, it's a first step, a jumping off spot for relationship and greater depth."

Alan knew the step between meeting neighbors and inviting them directly into his home was too much, too quick for many neighbors. So Free Coffee Friday became about creating a scene outside his house with the desire eventually to invite people in. As a result, Alan and his wife now invite these people into their home for dinner parties. One person, who showed up most every Friday, eventually began doing dinner with them, and two years later she became a Christian.

Should you do Taco Tuesday? Free Coffee Friday? Watermelon Wednesday? Meatloaf Monday? (Should we go on or do you get the point? 'Cause we could go all day!) Smoked-meat Sunday? Tea Thursday? (Okay, we'll stop for real.)

Game Nights

Hosting a regular game night is another low-stress way to invite others into deeper relationship (and into your home). Most people enjoy playing some kind of games, and doing this requires very little preparation—just get out the box or deck of cards and open the door!

Feel free to do what you enjoy with this as well, because that will give you the most motivation to stick with it. For example, I (Brandon) despise board games. I've never been interested in playing Monopoly or Settlers of Catan. However, I love any type of card games. I can play Uno or spades all day. So while I wouldn't likely succeed at starting a board game rhythm in my home, I quite enjoy having people over to play spades.

Remember my (Dustin's) story from chapter 2 about how I wanted my backyard exclusively to serve my desire for relaxation? Well, something ironic happened. I never actually bought that hammock I dreamed about so much. Instead, through the Holy Spirit's conviction, I invested in a Ping-Pong table and bocce ball set.

Not that there is anything wrong with having a hammock (I still want one!), but God impressed on me that a hammock would be all about me and my comfort, whereas looking at our home through a lens of hospitality would lead us to purchase games that others could enjoy with us. The cool thing about that backyard was that in many ways it was where the culture of our church plant began to thrive. We relentlessly hosted parties and had people over, and over a lot of homemade ice cream and cornhole, a community was birthed.

TV Shows

It's no secret that people are passionate about TV shows. These shows are a frequent topic of discussion around the watercooler at work, and odds are you understand why people love them so much. Stories are compelling; they make us think about life and they entertain and inspire us.

So if all that is true, it makes sense that we would use TV shows as an opportunity to do something together, to build commonality and enjoy something with others rather than by ourselves, isolated in our homes. So leverage these shows you enjoy, and offer your home as a place to watch them. Get some good food/snacks/drinks and provide an environment for people to hang out before or after, if they want to.

I (Brandon) have friends at my church who have done this for years with the popular show *The Walking Dead*. They watch it together and invite non-Christians to attend their watch parties. This has been a fruitful avenue for hospitality, and after all, what could be better than screaming in fear over flesh-eating zombies with a group of friends old and new? As an added benefit, most good TV shows center around themes like redemption, struggle, and forgiveness—and over time those themes can become great inroads to the gospel in a noncheesy way.

Watching Sports

People love their sports. Just as with TV shows, sports provide an avenue for us to watch things together that we'd typically watch alone. So whatever the big sport is where you live, you could leverage that for hospitality. Invite neighbors or coworkers over to watch the big game (or even the small games!).

Where I (Dustin) live, college football is the most widely loved sport. Every fall, I have Christian friends who open their homes all day on Saturdays to host watching parties for their network of relationships. This is a perfect opportunity for hospitality, and it makes for some lively banter when you have fans from different teams in the same room. Even though it can be helpful to choose a popular sport where you live, if you are going to do this regularly, you'll want to pick a sport you enjoy and focus on inviting others who also enjoy it.

Play Dates

Parents who are home alone with their kids a lot are often interested in spending time with other moms or dads who are also home alone with their kids. Play dates with other parents can be a helpful way to invite others into your home and also to keep you from going crazy!

Because of my (Brandon's) and my wife's work schedules, I am home alone with our kids for twelve hours on Fridays, and I often tell people that this day is without a doubt the hardest thing I do all week. I love my kids and enjoy spending time with them, but being alone with three kids all under age three for that amount of time is a challenge. So I guarantee you, if another dad invited us to his house on a Friday so the kids could play together, I am packing the stroller and heading there—if for no other reason than to have someone else share the crazy for a while and to be able to use the restroom without wondering if the kids are going to hurt one another.

Even something as simple as a play date can be an incredible opportunity.

Host Other Christians

We have focused a lot on using hospitality as a way to build relationships with non-Christians, but we also want to reiterate that the Scriptures call us to show hospitality to other Christians. First Peter 4:9 says, "Show hospitality to one another without grumbling." The "one another" here refers to others who also believe the gospel.[1] Sharing meals together, bearing one another's burdens, praying for one another, and confessing sin to one another during ordinary weeks in our ordinary homes is what it means to be the church.

One of the beneficial things about practicing hospitality with Christians is that we already have small groups from our local churches that provide easy opportunities to invite non-Christians in when the time is right. It helps to have this type of Christian community that meets in one another's homes and seeks to practice what we see in the book of Acts, in which the church community was fully invested in one another's lives (Acts 2:42–47).

For the record, we know this is a big ask to host people every week in your home. For example, my (Brandon's) small group meets at our home every Thursday night. We get home from long work days and then have twenty-something people show up (not including the twelve kids we have who also come). We wrap up right when our kids are falling apart from exhaustion and ready to go to bed. To be sure, this is a sacrifice, but it's one we believe is infinitely worth the cost. We get to watch people be honest with others for the first time and see Jesus bring about healing in those who are hurting. This community has become a place where we walk through life's good, bad, and ugly while reminding one another of the gospel. And as an added benefit, our kids grow up knowing that "church" is not only what happens on Sunday mornings, but what takes place on Thursday nights—and every moment.

We've also found that having Christians in our homes regularly piques the interest of our neighbors because it's so rare for people to regularly have groups at their houses. We've had numerous neighbors ask us, "What do you do on Thursday nights?" We have one neighbor couple who have become good friends of ours, and before we knew them, one Thursday they happened to walk by our house when people were arriving. Evidently when someone opened the door, the rest of us inside yelled, "Hey!"

A few weeks later my wife, Kristi, met the other neighbor wife, Katy. She asked Kristi what we were doing that night. Kristi told her, and Katy said, "Oh, gotcha. To be honest, it reminded me of a Bud Light commercial—the way everyone cheered when the person walked in." I feel like, "Have more Christian gatherings that could be confused with a Bud Light commercial" is a good goal for us as Christians.

MONTHLY RHYTHMS

There are certain rhythms that probably won't feasibly fit into a weekly routine, but may be more doable as a monthly or bimonthly practice. Consider some of the following ideas.

Neighborhood Cookouts

As I mentioned previously, while Renie and I (Dustin) were settling into our home in Atlanta and as part of hitting the reset button on our relationships with neighbors, we decided to implement once-a-month cookouts in our cul-de-sac. We found that many of our neighbors were interested in something like this, but they wouldn't initiate it.

Our neighbors directly across the street were from Russia and did not speak great English, but they always smiled while at the mailbox. Although we invited them repeatedly, they wouldn't come over. They would send their kids with incredible homemade bread to share, but the parents wouldn't show. Finally, through much convincing, Renie persuaded them to join us. Knowing this would be their first experience, I decided to step up the cuisine. Instead of the normal burgers, I would grill smoked pork ribs.

That evening, as they approached the cookout carrying baskets filled with homemade bread, in grand fashion, I opened the grill lid to showcase the sight and smell of the beautiful slow-cooked pork ribs, hoping it would impress them. And boy, did it make an impression.

While everyone pigged out on that luscious, tender meat, no one from the Russian family touched it—and their stay at the cookout was extremely short-lived. Turns out our Russian neighbors were Muslim. And Muslims do not eat pork products—including beautiful, smoked ribs. So that was great.

After my unfortunate failure, I noticed they no longer smiled as much when they walked to their mailbox. But God is gracious, and in due time we built a great relationship with them. In fact, we ended up, along with two other neighbors, being the only non-Muslim people they invited to their eldest daughter's wedding reception.

The entire ceremony was in Russian—except for the host's one English announcement: "Now the neighbors will speak."

About five hundred pairs of eyes looked at Renie and me. Surprised and stunned, we made our way to the stage and spoke a simple blessing over the newlyweds' lives. Because of a monthly neighborhood cookout, and despite the blunder of serving pork, God provided us with new friends, with whom we could speak Christian truths at a Muslim wedding.

Throw Parties (That People Want to Come To)

I (Brandon) have new next-door neighbors. They are a young family I've met only once, but I know they host great parties. I often pull up in our driveway, get out of my car, and immediately smell the charcoal and hear the booming laughter coming from their back deck.

Do you know what runs through my mind when this happens? *Man, that looks like so much fun. I wonder how I can get invited to one of their parties?* The reality is that I don't need to—I can host one of my own! You, too, can host parties that may make your neighbors wonder what they can do to get invited.

Although early in our marriage, Renie and I (Dustin) were not great at practicing hospitality with our immediate neighbors, we were in the rhythm of throwing monthly parties for different groups from our church. I am an enormous college sports fan, but my loyalty lies with the Clemson Tigers (my alma mater). God in His great humor gave me the opportunity to plant and pastor a church in Columbia, South Carolina—the home of Clemson's archrival, the South Carolina Gamecocks. As our church began to grow, we saw athletes from the university attending our services, which was a challenge, since everything in me wanted to see them lose every game. (Let's be real, God has a plethora of ways to sanctify us.)

A girl named Kate, who pitched for the university's softball team, was part of our church and consistently invited her teammates to come to our worship gatherings, but to no avail. Finally, Renie and I decided to partner with Kate to throw a party for the team at our home, as they had just won their way into the regional tournament.

It was simple. We had food and music, and we made homemade signs that wished them well. I even wore a "South Carolina Softball" T-shirt that night (it still pains me to think about it).

Out of this party, we made connections and began hosting regular get-togethers for the whole team. We felt as though we had become the team parents, and our end goal was not that they would eventually come to church to hear me preach, but that they would know that we cared for them and that Jesus cared for them deeply as well. One particular girl named Chrissy won our hearts and eventually she did attend a worship service. It just so happened that we were baptizing a bunch of other college students that night. With all our baptism gatherings, we allow the person who is getting baptized to share their story on video of how the gospel changed them.

Chrissy sat with tears flowing as she listened to story after story about Jesus and the forgiveness He offers. His grace was unlike any other news she had ever heard, and after the service she ran to me and said, "I want what they have and I want it right now." I walked through the gospel with her and helped her understand what confession, faith, repentance, and forgiveness look like. Sitting in an old, metal folding chair, God saved Chrissy that night.

As we finished praying, I could hear the water being drained from the portable baptistry, so I yelled to some volunteers to stop. That night, right there in her designer jeans and fancy shirt, Chrissy climbed into that pool and confessed publicly to a couple hundred people who were still gathered that Jesus was her Lord. It was incredible.

Chrissy is now a college softball coach in another part of the country, and six years later we still keep in touch with her as she now influences others. Though this story obviously does not mean that every act of hospitality will lead to salvation, you never know when a simple monthly party might lead to a baptism party that carries eternal significance.

Book Clubs

We've already mentioned this so we won't spend much time on it, but people love to read and they love to talk about what they read. So book clubs make a lot of sense. Also, people like an excuse to get together and talk. In Renie's book club, they often discuss the book for ten minutes and then hang out for the next hour and a half. If you like to read and know others who do too, this is a great opportunity.

Supper Clubs

Supper clubs are where you get a group of people and rotate hosting dinner at one another's houses. The host can provide the meal or you can do more of a potluck style. Either way, supper clubs can be a great opportunity to connect with people over a great meal. This idea could also function as a good second step, or something to pursue after you've already had someone in your home once, since it's a little more involved.

Movie Nights

Hosting neighborhood movie nights is a brilliant way to invite people over, and the more fun you can make it, the better. Doing it outside, if possible, is a win as well, because then it becomes visible for others who may walk by. You can buy an old projector fairly inexpensively and use a bed sheet to create a fun atmosphere. But also your trusty old TV in your living room along with some bowls of popcorn can work just as well!

Neighborhood Groups or Events

Maybe you occasionally get a flyer in your mailbox about an event happening in your neighborhood and you think, *Why would I go to that?* But when you practice a lifestyle of gospel-driven hospitality, you now have a reason to go! Participating in things that your neighbors are already doing is a simple way to make relationships and be a good neighbor. This can also include neighborhood clubs or gardens, HOA events, or even on-campus clubs, if you are a college student.

Reverse Hospitality

Reverse hospitality is when you take something to someone else's house to bless them. This can be delivering soup to your ill neighbor, providing a meal to a family who just brought home a newborn, or taking cookies to someone who just moved in down the street.

This idea is also about accepting the hospitality and generosity of others, because sometimes letting your neighbor serve you is one of the best ways you can build a foundation for relationship. For instance, you could ask your neighbor to help you move something that's heavy in hopes that one day when your neighbor needs help lugging a big piece of furniture up the stairs, they'll knock on your door.

We have a friend who jokes that he has a "ministry of borrowing tools" from his neighbors. Borrowing tools he doesn't have (and returning them better than he found them) lets his neighbors bless him instead of always seeking ways to serve them in a one-sided way.

YEARLY RHYTHMS

Some of the best opportunities for hospitality happen on a less frequent basis, and can function as incredible inroads for relationships. Consider these options.

Once-a-Year Events

Big annual events are a great excuse to gather people together and throw parties. The Super Bowl is a no-brainer, of course, because everyone watches the Super Bowl, if for nothing else but the commercials. Hosting a well-done, fun Super Bowl party for friends and neighbors is an incredible way to provide momentum for a lifestyle of hospitality.

The same holds true for other big sporting events, as well as awards shows. The Grammys, the Emmys, the Oscars, and the Tonys are perfect avenues for viewing parties. And don't forget events that happen less frequently—the World Cup or the Olympics. Just the other week I (Brandon) went to a Tony Awards viewing party that one of our church members hosted. I was encouraged to see them leverage their home for this purpose and loved being able to connect with non-Christians I may not ever otherwise get to meet.

Holiday Parties

Holidays offer a perfect reason to get people together and celebrate. Whether it's an ugly sweater Christmas party, a pre-Thanksgiving neighborhood potluck, or a fiesta for Cinco de Mayo (who doesn't like a reason to eat Mexican food?)—any holiday is an opportunity for hospitality.

Fireworks are obviously a thing for New Year's and July Fourth, so feel free to spend lots of money on fireworks and invite others over to enjoy the show (obviously make sure it's legal in your state and then set them up correctly).

> When strategizing over what might work best for your particular context, try to learn the rhythms of those who live around you.

This past New Year's I (Dustin) went in with some friends to create the biggest fireworks show in the neighborhood. Renie and I were originally hosting the party, but my friend Vince decided he wanted to be the hospitable one that night. That was a big mistake.

In the spirit of "go big or go home" I purchased the most powerful fireworks I could buy: mortars. Vince accidentally set them up sideways. I didn't notice before he lit them, but as the fuse caught, I realized this potential disaster.

Fourteen screaming balls of fire shot out like little cannons, and half of them took dead aim at the neighbor's house directly across the street. It felt as if we had declared war on them. These neighbors, whom Vince had never met, also happened to have a newborn sleeping in the front room where the fireworks made their direct hit. To say the least, Vince met the neighbors that night. So when all else fails when trying to meet your neighbors, just shoot fireworks at their house, I guess.

When strategizing over what might work best for your particular context, try to learn the rhythms of those who live around you. What holidays do your neighbors go all out for? Is the neighborhood booming on Halloween, but fairly quiet at Christmastime? Is there a parade for the Fourth of July but everyone is out of town for Thanksgiving? Knowing this will help you figure out where to focus your efforts.

For years my (Dustin's) family's tendency has been to make the trek to be with our extended families on Easter. But we discovered that none of our non-Christian friends or neighbors leave town that weekend. In an effort to practice hospitality, we committed to stay in town for Easter weekends so we can host a party on Saturday (with an Easter egg hunt for the kids, of course). Then we have a more formal Sunday lunch with all of our non-Christian friends and neighbors.

As we started doing this, surprisingly most of our neighbors have attended our church's Easter celebration service. It seems that as we have invited them into our lives, they have a growing desire to experience what is important to us—like Easter. Some of our best gospel conversations come on Easter weekends around our table. There is no better way to use hospitality as an inroad to the gospel than to talk about the empty tomb on Easter Sunday.

Create Your Own Holidays

The more creative we can be, the more our neighbors and friends are intrigued to join us for something. If regular, "real" holidays don't work out, try creating your own holidays. Celebrate National Pancake Day or National Pizza Day—or just make up something. Creating your own celebrations can be a benefit because (a) it is unusual, and (b) you don't have to compete with other holiday events, because you made it up. Be honest, if you're a *Seinfeld* fan, you've always wanted to have your own version of Festivus, like Kramer did, right? (Festivus was a made-up holiday, celebrated on December 23, that was an alternative to the consumerism of Christmas.)

My (Dustin's) friend Matt created a yearly holiday, which he refers to as First Friday. Every autumn, in the southeastern part of the United States, college football becomes a way of life. First Friday is simply the first Friday before the Saturday kickoff of the college football season. Matt began hosting this celebration—complete with "tailgate food" like wings, chips, dips, sliders, and boiled peanuts (yes, boiled)—his first year out of college, and fourteen years later, more than a hundred people now attend.

I (Dustin) have copycatted the idea and now throw my own First Friday holiday celebration.

Of course, you don't have to create holidays that attract a hundred people, as Matt has, but you *can* get creative and have fun with it and see what God might do through your simple creativity and a desire to use your home.

Kids' Birthday Parties

If you have young kids, you know about kids' birthday parties. Depending on your circle of friends and your stage of life, you may think, *Oh, a kids' party. That sounds fun in a kiddie sort of way.* Or you may have been to forty-seven of them this year and you think, *Please don't make me go to another one of those!*

The thing is, kids' birthday parties don't have to be torture for adults (even though they often are). If you have a birthday party for your child, invite the parents you are building relationships with. They may graciously decline because they are sick to death of these parties, or they may gladly take you up on it because they want themselves and their kids to have more friends. Either way, you can do small things to make the party more enjoyable for the adults. Offer good adult food, with real plates and drinks, and not just prepackaged PB&Js with grape Kool-Aid. Put out a horseshoe set or cornhole set (dads especially seem to love this adult beanbag toss game). Maybe even get a tournament going. Take turns watching the kids so the adults can have a break and talk to one another rather than just chase their hyped-up-on-sugar kids around.

The bottom line is, you're probably going to have a birthday party for your children, so why not turn that normal event into something intentional for the sake of hospitality?

MAKING THE IDEAS A REALITY

The ideas we mentioned in this chapter are just that—ideas. There are endless hospitable rhythms you can implement into your life, and we hope that these have either encouraged you to copy them or inspired you to dream up your own.

Spend some time looking back through the ideas we presented and pray about what rhythms of hospitality God may be leading you to pursue.

QUESTIONS TO CONSIDER

- Which of the weekly, monthly, or yearly rhythms presented in this chapter is most appealing to you? Which ones do you think would work best where you live, work, and play?
- What normal events could you turn into a means of practicing hospitality? Which event is the next one on the calendar— maybe a kid's birthday party or a holiday? What would you do to infuse this event with purpose and mission?
- How can the love of Christians for other Christians allow outsiders to catch a glimpse of the gospel? How might these same relationships cause followers of Jesus to neglect showing hospitality to those who are far from God?

CHAPTER 10

HOW DO YOU GET TO THE GOSPEL?

The end goal of hospitality is not that you simply host people in your home as much as you use your home as a place to display and speak the gospel. Paul, who repeatedly pointed us to the practice of hospitality[1] also boldly proclaimed his desire to be valiant about the good news of the gospel: "I am not ashamed of the gospel, for it is the power of God for salvation to everyone who believes" (Rom. 1:16).

Clearly the aim of hospitality is more than merely inviting someone into our home, sharing a good meal and a few stories, and calling it a night. We are missionaries, after all. Paul reminded us, "We are ambassadors for Christ, God making his appeal through us" (2 Cor. 5:20). And pastor Charles Spurgeon said, "Every Christian . . . is either a missionary or an imposter."[2]

Our mission, as ambassadors of Christ, is to share the good news of Jesus' work through His life, death, burial, and resurrection. This is the true hope for the world. As a result, we can't keep from speaking the gospel to those we love—or at least we should not be able to.

THE GOOD NEWS IS MOTIVATING

I (Dustin) remember vividly the weeks following my conversion when I could not help but talk about Jesus. I was young but bold, and the change in me was real. I had a new heart and I could not help but tell those around me about it. Everyone who knows Jesus has a story of how He rescued us—how He helped us see our folly and need for Him and brought us to Himself.

As a Christian, you were dead and were made alive—and will live forever. You believed and confessed and, as a result, you are saved. Our salvation is the fuel that fans the flames of a hospitable lifestyle.

God has changed your life, and you long for others to experience that same transformation. You know that if they believe and confess then they, too, can come to know Christ's goodness, satisfaction, and eternal love. Think about that for a moment—the coworker who gets under your skin, the neighbor whose dog won't stop barking, or the stranger you meet at the bus stop—these people can be saved and enjoy an eternity of God's hospitality, all because of the work Jesus has done. And you can be part of helping that to happen.

THE GOOD NEWS IS HOPE, NOT ADVICE

The world's overwhelming answer to hurt or pain or sorrow or disappointment is "do better, try harder, be good, stop making bad choices . . ." and the list of advice goes on and on. Dr. Phil and Oprah have made a fortune off these concepts alone. We can safely assume that these are the voices that shape the worldview of those who will be sitting around our tables. They understand life in these terms and deal with their failures by following these principles.

> People are way more eager to hear about God's grace than we are to speak of it.

Thankfully you understand this worldview. Apart from God's grace, you likely also lived according to these mantras and false hopes. In reality you have much in common with your neighbors and those you rub shoulders with daily, because at the core we are all sinners in need of Jesus. If you see your neighbors and friends in this light, you will be motivated to share the life-changing hope of the gospel.

That is because the gospel is altogether different from the views of most. The gospel is not advice for how to live, but rather an announcement of good news. And this perfect One died to pay the price our sin deserved and offers us a relationship with the true and living God. This is the hope we have the opportunity to share with our friends, neighbors, and coworkers—and it's much better news than the pressure-filled mantras they are used to turning to. The gospel has the opposite effect from the white-knuckling, behavior-modification-focused advice—because the gospel states that the perfect behavior of Jesus is what saves us, not our own efforts. What a freeing, revolutionary concept grace is!

Yes, as you take the bold step of speaking the good news, you may feel nervous and reluctant for fear that you will be rejected, but understand that the gospel you have is so attractive to the hurting who live right next door to you. It is the *good news* their souls long for deep down, even if they resist it. The more you share this good news, the more you will discern how hungry people actually are for it. People are way more eager to hear about God's grace than we are to speak of it.

HOW TO MAKE THE MOST IMPACT

We encourage you to speak the truth of the gospel any and every chance you get. As you do so, we also encourage you to share with grace and understanding. So we have a few tips and insights that will help you share more successfully.

Avoid the Bait-and-Switch Approach

Everyone hates this. Someone asks to drop by because he hasn't seen you in a while. You anticipate a casual conversation with an old buddy. After a few minutes of polite banter, he abruptly changes the conversation: "What I really wanted to tell you is that I've started a job selling dinner knives. I'd love to show you the sheer magnificence and cutting power of this bad boy." *No!*

Not only do you not want to see the knife, but you feel manipulated. Your buddy fed you a line to get in the door, knowing full well that all he wanted to do was hawk his product. Wouldn't it be better if he were just up-front with his motives in the first place?

The same is true for our efforts at biblical hospitality. The first time you have a new friend into your home, it's rarely wise to declare, "Well, new friend, you know the real reason we had you guys over is so that I could tell you a few things about God." This type of backdoor approach feels as manipulative to your neighbors as the knife salesman feels to you. Not only that, but you may lose any later chance to winsomely speak of the gospel.

Avoid Forced Presentations

Not all gospel presentations are bad, so we aren't suggesting that you not go that route.[3] Keep in mind, however, that using these presentations over a meal rarely feels natural or authentic.

If after thirty minutes of postdinner conversation you break out your gospel tract, your actions may have the same effect as the bait-and-switch approach, except now you appear like the marketer of a chain of time-shares at the beach. "You have to listen to my presentation if you want dessert, buddy. We're not letting you out of this house to enjoy your night unless you grin and bear it."

Hospitality is not a new program or the latest evangelism kit, but an ancient practice and a way of life. There is no need to overcomplicate this idea or force it into a preprogrammed package. As author David Platt said,

> If we were left to ourselves with the task of taking the gospel to the world, we would immediately begin planning innovative strategies and plotting elaborate schemes. We would organize conventions, develop programs, and create foundations. . . . But Jesus is so different from us. With the task of taking the gospel to the world, he wandered through the streets and byways. . . . All he wanted was a few men who would think as he did, love as he did, see as he did, teach as he did, and serve as he did. All he needed was to revolutionize the hearts of a few, and they would impact the world.[4]

Learn how to speak the gospel naturally in the overall flow of relationship, and your friends and neighbors are much more likely to listen attentively. If they can tell that you love them and believe what you are saying, you've gained credibility and gotten their interest.

Consider the "I Have Good News for You" Test

If you really believe that the gospel is good news, it will show in your life and will be applicable to the real struggles your friends and neighbors mention. Internalize the gospel in such a way that you work its truths into all types of conversations. One quick tool is to check and see if the statements you say still work if you put the words *I have good news for you* in front of them.

For example, if you know a neighbor is dealing with loneliness, does it work to say, "I have good news for you: you really need to get better at making friends if you feel so lonely"? No, of course not. However, does it work if you say, "I have good news for you: I hate that you feel lonely, and I think God hates that too. Maybe part of the reason we met is because He loves you and wants you to have a new friend"? Yep, that's good news. That's a way to insert gospel truth into conversations naturally, without a forced or awkward presentation.

One more: if you have a coworker over for dinner, and he mentions that his marriage is in a rocky place, does it work for you to say, "I have good news for you: if you weren't a heathen sinner, your marriage probably wouldn't be this bad"? Nope. Not good news for him. However, if you were to respond, "I have good news for you: I believe God created marriage to teach us how much He loves us, and that even when it's hard, we can find beauty in His design. I'd love to talk with you more about that and help in whatever way I can"? Yep, that passes the test!

Learning how to speak of the gospel naturally and apply it as good news to people's real issues may take work. But over time you are likely to be surprised at how well you do.[5]

Avoid Lovelessness

Obviously, we know that people are not objects for us to use so we feel better about ourselves or to prove that we've been obedient for once. Our neighbors have great intuition—they know when they are being used. If we rush through a conversation to get to a point we are trying to make, people will know that we don't really care about them.

Sure, some may reject the gospel, but that does not mean that God is not at work.

Our friend Matt, who is a pastor, recently told us a story about avoiding lovelessness.

> One Sunday I was preaching on evangelism, and in the course of the message, I shared a story about my attempts to love a neighbor whom God had placed on my heart. I emphasized how little I had in common with this neighbor, making a couple jokes about how challenging it was for me to find points of commonality with him. Then I proceeded to publicly pat myself on the back by declaring that I had pushed through my fears and boldly spoken the gospel to this pagan. (I didn't use the word *pagan*, but the implication was clear.) Once I finished my story I looked up, and to my horror, this neighbor was sitting in the third row. He had finally taken my invitation to come and check out our church—just in time for me to mock him and exalt myself.

We can all be guilty of this type of loveless folly. We discuss our unsaved friends as though they are targets. We tell stories about them to flaunt our obedience. We share prayer requests designed to make them look bad so that others will be impressed that we'd invite someone like *that* into our homes. In so doing, we epitomize Paul's principle that without love we are merely a clanging cymbal.[6] Who wants to have dinner with someone like that? The aim of hospitality is to forge relationships strong enough to bear the weight of truth, but our relationships will never get to that point if we do not offer genuine love.

GETTING TO THE GOSPEL

Assuming you've avoided the aforementioned land mines, let's move on to how you shape everyday normal conversations into life-giving gospel conversations.

Trust that God Goes Before You

The nature and character of God is your greatest help when practicing hospitality. You can rest assured that God goes before you. He has been preparing the hearts of those you will engage. Sure, some may reject the gospel, but that does not mean that God is not at work. You never know how your hospitality may play a role in those people being receptive to the gospel ten years from now. Whether they trust in Christ at the first meal or many years later, we can rest in God's sovereignty, trusting that He desires—far more than we ever could—for our friends and neighbors to accept Him.

Let the truth expressed in Deuteronomy 31:8 be a grounding reality for you: "The LORD himself goes before you and will be with you; he will never leave you nor forsake you. Do not be afraid; do not be discouraged" (NIV).

I (Brandon) realized this about my neighbor Stuart, which I shared in chapter 1. When he said, "I thought maybe God sent you to talk to me that day," it became very clear that God is at work ahead of us. We can join God in what He's already doing, and we can experience a lot of freedom and confidence in that.

Listen Carefully

We do have incredible news to share with the world, but it is essential to listen to and learn from the people we seek to love. The reality is that everyone knows that life is broken and they need some source of salvation to make their lives right and whole. They might find their hope in sports, money, marriage, pleasure, or any host of pseudogods. But we can rest assured, they have *something*. The key is to listen for these false sources of hope. These modern-day idols are merely the pursuits to fix the brokenness that all of humanity feel and experience.

Be attentive to the places of pain that exist in their lives. Jesus is in the business of healing, so find their wounds, care for them, and watch Jesus cure their souls. Listen when they share the things that bring them joy. Listen when they talk about what they hope for the future. When people allude to these aspects, ask more questions and seek greater clarity. These types of conversational markers are like big rocks in a muddy river. Kick them over and you never know what you might find.

As you simply listen well, you practice Christ's compassion. The world is full of people who halfway listen to others just so they can take their turn talking next. When we forsake this shallow self-interest and focus on truly hearing and understanding others, we model the truth that God sees us, hears us, and knows our troubles.[7] Loving and following a compassionate God will produce compassion in us for those we encounter.

Ask Good Questions

Good questions aid you in understanding your neighbor's heart. We've probably all been in conversations with someone when it was clear that they were not really listening to what we were saying. At a break in the conversation, when it would make sense for them to ask you a question, they ask the most random, off-the-wall, unrelated question you've ever heard. Conversation over!

Or perhaps you've met the person who has the unique ability to kill every conversation by asking questions that go nowhere: "So you've been married five months?"

"Yes." . . .

Awkward!

Instead consider arming yourself with simple questions that foster further conversation. Before Renie and I (Dustin) were having people over to dinner for the first time, no lie, I sat with my journal and wrote question after question to ask them, and then went over those questions again and again.

That night went well, and I only had to resort to a couple questions before we found some common ground. The questions got everything going and worked well as a starting point.

The point is, doing hospitality well and asking strong questions that lead the conversation takes time and practice, but it's worth the effort because it offers them the opportunity to share something they might not normally would have.

Make sure, though, you ask open-ended questions, because nothing is more frustrating than asking something that the person can simply give a yes or no response to. You have to train yourself at asking these types of questions until it becomes a natural rhythm.

> Let them be the focal point. Then when they turn the conversation toward you, be intentional.

They can be as simple as, "Can you tell me more about that?" or, "That's interesting. I've never thought of it that way. What makes you think that?" Open-ended, leading questions drive the conversation forward, demonstrating that you are genuinely interested and listening. Try questions like:

- How long have you lived here? What's your experience been so far?
- Do you have pets? Tell me about them.
- What's your favorite sports team? How did you begin cheering for them?
- What's your favorite local restaurant? How often do you get to go?
- Do you have kids? How many? What are their personalities like?
- What do you like about this area? What would you change?
- Where did you grow up? What was your childhood like?
- What kind of hobbies do you like? ·
- What is your favorite movie? Music? TV show?
- What do you do for work? What's your favorite part about your job?

If you already know certain things about the people you are having over, do some quick research on what you know about them so you can ask better questions. For example, one time I (Dustin) knew that a neighbor was Wiccan, so I did a quick Google search to figure out some questions based around her beliefs—not in a demeaning way, but rather in a loving way to show that I was interested.

Tell Your Story

Hospitality presents a wonderful way to get to know other people —and what do people do when they get to know one another? They tell stories. Your neighbors will do this. They will tell you where they grew up, went to college, and met their spouse. They will likely tell you about significant details that shaped them into the man and woman they are today. Then it's your turn.

But please, wait your turn and do not be "Captain One Up." If they went on a trip to the Caribbean, refrain from telling them you have been to the Caribbean seventeen times in the last five years.

Let them be the focal point. Then when they turn the conversation toward you, be intentional. This is a softball pitch for you to hit out of the park. After all, the most significant part of your life is the work Jesus has done to transform you. You'll be able to share about the person you were before you met Jesus, how He saved you, and what He is doing in your life now.

Don't waste this opportunity by rambling about silly, nonessential things. Don't be so scared of the bait and switch that you don't talk about the most important thing in your life. Speak up. Tell your story. Trust God with the rest.

Talk about Jesus

We heard a story from a small group leader that illustrates a problem many Christians have. This leader found that the members of his group were super awkward when it came to talking about Jesus. They'd act as though they were at a middle-school dance every time it came up. So one night he began their meeting by saying, "On the count of three, we are all going to say Jesus' name ten times."

His point was clear. Jesus should not be hard for Christians to talk about. Jesus isn't a crazy uncle we want to keep hidden at the family reunion. He's our Savior and Lord. He's the most important person in our lives. Because this is true, talking about Him should be second nature, like talking about our favorite sports team or band. Yes, some of your neighbors may think you're a bit weird, but who cares? Pastor and author Russell Moore says, "As Christianity seems increasingly strange, and even subversive, to our culture, we have the opportunity to reclaim the freakishness of the gospel, which is what gives it its power in the first place."[8]

Our friends Micah and Laurie, who live out hospitality, were recently having dinner with some friends, Clark and Mallory, whom they'd initially met by throwing a block party in their neighborhood. Through more than a year of building a strong relationship, many meals, and a lot of sitting together on their deck while their kids played, Clark and Mallory eventually became part of a weekly small group that meets in the neighborhood, and they even host it at their house from time to time. Neither of them is a believer, yet through the gateway of hospitality, they are now reading the Bibles that Micah and Laurie gave them.

The group is currently discussing the book of Revelation (we do not recommend this as the first book of the Bible you bring up with the people you have over!) and talking about Jesus' return. Mallory had no idea that Jesus was coming back one day and that those who believed in Him would experience no more pain and no more tears.[9] She said, "If all of this is really true and Jesus really is coming back one day, then why don't you talk about this more?"

The interesting part is that Micah and Laurie talk about the gospel with both Clark and Mallory on an almost-weekly basis, and yet they were asking for more. That admission should speak volumes to those of us who carry this incredible news.

Our desire is not to guilt you into talking about Revelation with your friends or being the annoying Christian who wears T-shirts with odd sayings on them. We want to encourage you toward speaking boldly about Jesus through genuine love and concern for others. Most people value authenticity, so they'd rather you speak about things that you love than keep them hidden.

Additionally, some of Scripture's primary metaphors about our spiritual need are actually those of hunger and thirst. Isaiah 55:1–3 is one such passage that poignantly describes God as the only true source of satisfaction for humanity, yet acknowledges He is the last place we look for satisfaction in our broken state.

> Come, everyone who thirsts, come to the waters; and he who has no money, come, buy and eat! Come, buy wine and milk without money and without price. Why do you spend your money for that which is not bread, and your labor for that which does not satisfy? Listen diligently to me, and eat what is good, and delight yourselves in rich food. Incline your ear, and come to me; hear, that your soul may live.

As you gather with people over food and drink that replenish your physical needs, you will often hear about what others think meet their spiritual needs. You'll find out what particular things have become "that which is not bread" for them—money, control, approval, sex, power, or comfort—the things that will never truly satisfy them. This knowledge gives you a perfect opportunity to speak the truth that God not only created the desires they seek to fill, but that He alone can fill them. Gathering around food and drink is the most ideal time to talk about Jesus and ask piercing questions from the mouth of God, such as Isaiah 55:2: "Why do you spend your money for that which is not bread, and your labor for that which does not satisfy?"

Keep It Going

You are likely going to get more than one opportunity to speak to your neighbors. That's the beauty of developing rhythms of hospitality. You are likely to see them the next day on the way to work or when they're taking their dog for a walk. This allows you to keep the relationship, and the conversation, going. In fact, you might imagine a yearlong relationship with a friend or neighbor like one big, ongoing conversation. Each time you meet, pick up where you left off. This means you need to remember essential points in the conversation.

This may seem weird to you, but embrace it. We have a friend who uses the notes app on his phone to keep records of his conversations with neighbors. It helps him pray for them specifically as well as allows him to look back at the notes when he knows he's likely to see them again. If they speak of pain, then you have a built-in chance to say, "Hey, I'd love to hear how things are going with that situation you mentioned last night. I prayed this morning that God would provide for your needs."

If you are like us, you are also likely to think of things you wished you had said once the night was over. You remember a great story or think of an inroad to the gospel that you missed. Well, guess what? You've got another chance. Since the person is still in your life, you can simply spin back into the conversation: "You know, after you left last night, I had another thought about that thing you mentioned . . ." Just like that, you are right back in the flow of the conversation and you can keep it going time and time again.

There's no one right way to speak about Jesus. The important thing is that you take advantage of any opportunity biblical hospitality presents. Thankfully, God will take our feeble efforts, multiply them, and bring far greater results than we can ask or imagine.

QUESTIONS TO CONSIDER

- How should your salvation motivate you to live a hospitable life?
- Which of the practical tips for moving a conversation to the gospel comes most naturally for you? Which of these tips is most challenging? What steps could you take to grow in these weaker areas?

- How does your view of mission and hospitality change with the knowledge that God goes before you, lives inside you, and accomplishes the work for you? How should these truths encourage and motivate you?

CHAPTER 11

OTHER WAYS TO LEVERAGE YOUR HOME FOR MISSION

Of course, there are more things you can do to practice hospitality than inviting others into your home for meals, parties, games, and ordinary life rhythms. Let's take a look at some of those additional ways to turn your home into a weapon for the gospel.

INVITE SINGLE PEOPLE INTO YOUR FAMILY RHYTHMS

If you are married and/or have children, you have a social-support system that single people do not have. Single people can have incredible and fulfilling community, but that does not mean they would not enjoy being invited into a nuclear family from time to time.

We would highly encourage every Christian family to be intentional about welcoming the single people of your church into the rhythms of your family, and maybe even informally "adopt" someone (only if they are interested, of course). Have them over for meals. Let them help put the kids to bed and read them bedtime stories. Invite them for holiday gatherings. Let them experience what life in your family is like, because (a) they will likely feel welcomed and loved, and (b) if one day they end up with a family of their own, their time with you may be formative in shaping how they relate to their spouse and children.

A family that I (Dustin) am friends with has consistently invited a single girl from their church to participate in their family rhythms. Recently they received this touching card from her:

> I just wanted to write a little note to tell you how thankful I am for you both! The card itself says a lot: "Every day we spend together is a day well spent!" I thoroughly enjoy spending time with you guys. I am always refreshed and encouraged by any amount of time that we spend together. You guys spur me on to know and love Jesus more! I am filled with joy because of the grace poured out to me that I get to be your friend!
>
> I would love to have a family of my own one day, and whether that happens or not, I am, and will be, okay—(1) because of Jesus, and (2) because I am loved and cared for by your family (and I feel a part of it)!
>
> So thank you for taking me in and being my friend. Thank you for loving me so well! I am beyond blessed by y'all and I thank the Lord for you guys.

You may not always realize it, but many times the single people in your church are struggling with their singleness and their unfulfilled desire for marriage and a family. God has designed the church such that these people—whether in a season or a lifetime of singleness—should never have to feel alone or adrift. We can share with them the gift of our families and enfold the lonely into community. This is an important call for those of us in the church who have families, so let's not look past it.

You can also apply this concept to any life stage. Welcoming those who are younger into your family is an incredible way to disciple them and give them a picture of what a godly man, woman, or family looks like—especially if they do not have that picture anywhere else. This might mean becoming intentional about welcoming into your family rhythms your kids' friends who don't have Christian families. If you are an older married couple, you may need to invite an engaged couple into your life, or offer any sort of mentoring by opening your life to another who may benefit from it.

CONNECT WITH A COUPLE
OR FAMILY (IF YOU ARE SINGLE)

This is the flip side of the previous point. Often there seems to be a natural disconnect where singles only hang out with other singles, and families only hang out with other families. This makes sense since we naturally congregate with those in our same life stage, but when we do this, we miss out on a lot of potential relationships both inside and outside the church.

Single folks: you may be tempted to believe that the married couples and families you know have all the cards. They are married, you are not. They have kids, you don't. They are a group, you're only one person. In light of that, if anyone is going to invite the other into their life, it should be them inviting you, right? I (Brandon) actually wouldn't argue that point, as I would love for families to take the lead in that. But I will tell you this: a lot of the assumptions you might make about your friends in a different life stage than you probably aren't true. You may think they are completely satisfied, with all their relational needs met because they are married and/or have cute little munchkins to cuddle. But your married friends or friends with kids would probably get a good laugh out of that. As a single friend of mine recently said, "I'm not half as lonely as most of my married friends are."

You may think they are disinterested in hanging out with you because they haven't made the first move, but that's likely not true. Rather, it's more likely they are so bone-tired from chasing their kids around they haven't thought about much else recently. Or honestly, some married couples just assume you wouldn't want to hang out with them—because you're still cool and single and free and they are none of the above. They think, *Would others really want to be with us while we watch mind-numbing cartoons, dodge toys hurtled through the air, and clean up whatever bodily fluid is coming out of our little ones at the time?*

So if you're open to it and interested, invite people outside your life stage into your life. It might surprise you how open others are to you engaging with them. Offer to take them dessert and play with

> We worship God when we open our homes to the widow.

the kids, or for them to join you at a local park. This is a great way to build deeper relationships in the church and also be intentional with families who are far from Jesus.

Our friend Caitlin is single and several years younger than my wife and me (Brandon), and she's become part of our family. She comes over for dinner, goes to baseball games with us, and even volunteers to watch our kids. Our kids love her and feel at home around her. That happened because Caitlin was willing to reach out and build a friendship with Kristi. We are honored that Caitlin actually wants to hang out with some lame parents covered in spit-up, and happy to have another adult around who says things other than, "Why?" and "What's that, Daddy?"

CARE FOR WIDOWS AND WIDOWERS

James 1:27 makes clear our call as Christians to care for widows: "Religion that is pure and undefiled before God the Father is this: to visit orphans and widows in their affliction, and to keep oneself unstained from the world."

The word *religion* in this passage means worship.[1] Therefore, we worship God when we open our homes to the widow. This is similar to our call to enfold single people into our families. Many widows and widowers would be delighted to spend time with you. In some cases, however, particularly if they are elderly, you will need to practice reverse hospitality, since they may be confined to their homes or care facilities. In our busy lives and fast-paced culture, older people are sometimes neglected, and it's easy to forget the pain of those who have recently experienced loss—but that shouldn't be the case for the church.

Mrs. Pat is eighty-four years young and has been without her husband for more than forty years. She and her husband never had children, but Mrs. Pat has not let that stop her from crocheting scarves for all the children in the local church and hundreds beyond her community through a ministry called Operation Christmas Child.

My (Dustin's) sister and her family invite Mrs. Pat over for many Sunday lunches, along with Mother's Day, Easter, birthdays, and any other excuse to make her part of their gang. I have had the privilege of meeting Mrs. Pat, and though we have apologized to her for how loud and obnoxious we can all be when we get together, she admits she likes the noise because of how quiet it can be around her home.

Though I live hours from her, when I recently had major surgery on my Achilles tendon, I received a card from none other than Mrs. Pat. There is no reason for any widow or widower within the church not to have family that they can make their own, and the starting point is often a simple invitation. There are so many Mrs. Pats out there who need to feel the warmth of biblical hospitality. We can honor these older saints by making a place at the table for them, and learn from their wisdom while we're at it.

SHELTER PEOPLE

Sometimes people, both inside and outside of the church, will need a place to stay temporarily. Maybe they are in transition and can't move into their next apartment yet, maybe they have financial troubles, or maybe it's some other reason. Offering a spare bed or couch to someone who could greatly benefit from it is a beautiful way to practice hospitality. When we move from thinking that we own our homes to the reality that God has given them to us to steward, it changes our entire perspective.

We both have had numerous people stay with us for short periods, and we both have had great and not-so-great experiences. But this openness has been a key part of developing a lifestyle of hospitality—because it doesn't get more real than having someone in your kitchen first thing in the morning (especially when you forgot they were there!). And if the church is designed to be family with one another, then temporary shelter certainly falls on the list of things that family would do for one another.

When we were pastoring together in South Carolina, we saw a beautiful example of this ministry. A young couple in our church, Eric and Kelly, got pregnant out of wedlock. Then they found out they were having triplets—something they were definitely not ready for.

So Denson and Jackie, an older couple in our church, offered to let Kelly move into their home. They even took an active role in making sure she got the medical care she needed.

Eric and Kelly wanted to get married but didn't have the money for a wedding, so the small group they were in planned a wedding for them. They tracked down a venue, decorations, and photographer. They even had a baby shower for them beforehand. This group threw them the most gorgeous wedding. It was a beautiful picture of God's people surrounding a couple in dire need of support, and a godly older couple who took in a pregnant mother, knowing that the reward was worth any inconvenience it caused them.

CARE FOR ORPHANS

As James 1:27 talks about caring for widows and widowers, it also states that caring for orphans is a mark of "religion that is pure and undefiled." The act of bringing a child into your family—whether through fostering or adoption—is obviously a clear way to practice hospitality.

> Our homes are not our own, but rather a weapon given to us to push back darkness and hold up light for the hurting.

Romans 15:7 says, "Welcome one another as Christ has welcomed you, for the glory of God." What is adopting or fostering a child if not the very act of welcoming an orphan into our family the same way Christ welcomed us spiritual orphans into His family?

There is a great need for orphan care around the world and also in our own backyards. Christians should lead the charge to be diligently hospitable to children in need. This is a beautiful and compelling act of hospitality that puts God's lavish hospitality to us on full display.

The number of children who need homes just in my (Dustin's) state is staggering.[2] I was recently encouraged to discover what one friend is doing about it. Faith is a single woman in her twenties. She is talented, educated, and creative. She has a wonderful job. Though she could pursue countless other things, she has decided that foster care is worth giving her life to.

For the last year she has fostered six-year-old Mason, embracing the difficulties of being a single mom so Mason won't be without a family. Faith rents a two-bedroom townhouse that meets all the state agency requirements in an area where Mason can attend a good school. Faith's journey testifies to the truth that our homes are not our own, but rather a weapon given to us to push back darkness and hold up light for the hurting.

OPEN YOUR DORM ROOM FOR HOSPITALITY

College is an incredible environment to practice hospitality. You will likely have no other time where such a concentrated number of people in your same life stage will live within steps of you. And believe it or not, you will likely never have as much free time as you do now. What better way to use that time than to partner with other Christians, building friendships with people from all over the globe, and inviting them into your life and dorm room for the sake of the gospel.

A large part of my (Dustin's) life trajectory was affected by a Christian college student who practiced hospitality. I was a Christian when I went to college, but I was at a crossroads of deciding what type of person I would be. Would I be serious about my faith or go the partying route? Would my career path be motivated by a desire to help others or by a desire to selfishly gain unlimited comfort for myself? It was at this crossroads that an older college student, Matt New (the same Matt who started the First Friday parties), invited me to a Bible study in his dorm room with other freshman guys. Over the course of that year, through a lot of pancakes and bacon (the way to my heart), God used Matt's hospitality to change the course of my life. We are still friends and I am grateful for Matt's decision to leverage his dorm room for the gospel.

INTENTIONALLY WELCOME NEIGHBORS FROM ABROAD

Imagine moving to a new country where people who look like you are a vast minority. You don't know the cultural customs or norms, you speak only a little of the language, and you aren't even sure how to accomplish basic things like finding the best place to shop for groceries or obtaining a driver's license.

Anywhere you go you feel the weight and the constant presence of your differentness. How welcome would it feel if a kind and thoughtful neighbor invited you to their house for dinner? If they asked you about your story and seemed genuinely interested, if instead of ignoring your presence, they acknowledged it and sought to understand who you are?

Christians, there is great need for cross-cultural ministry right here in our own backyards. People from all over the world are visiting and relocating to North America, and odds are, no matter where you live you see an increasing presence of people who don't look like you. This is a wonderful gospel opportunity.

Over and over the Scriptures, both in the Old and New Testaments, command us to care for the stranger and the sojourner. In Leviticus 19:34, God instructed the Israelites: "You shall treat the stranger who sojourns with you as the native among you, and you shall love him as yourself, for you were strangers in the land of Egypt: I am the LORD your God." This is a gospel-centered motivation for welcoming the stranger and foreigner by pointing out the fact that the Israelites were once strangers in need of welcoming as well.

In Matthew 25:31–46, when Jesus spoke of separating the sheep from the goats—the sheep being the ones who welcomed Him as a stranger, fed Him, and clothed Him—He stated, "I say to you, as you did it to one of the least of these my brothers, you did it to me" (v. 40). His point was that as we welcome the stranger, we welcome Christ Himself.

Regardless of our political stances on immigration, as Christians, we have no excuse for neglecting to welcome strangers and foreigners around us. We were once strangers who needed to be included and welcomed.[3] In light of that knowledge, we must do the same for others.

You can be a welcoming presence to the ethnic minority or immigrant families you come in contact with. You can volunteer to help international college students. You can even get involved with local refugee resettlement programs, which seek to connect refugees with host families to teach them basic things about the culture and be a relational resource to answer questions.

In the early days of the church we started together, we came across a homeless immigrant named Luis. He was the very definition of an outsider: he barely spoke English, he didn't fit in anywhere, and he didn't even have a place to live. But he had a great sense of humor and a bright smile, and despite how different he was, he wanted to be friends with our church members.

We watched our church family rally around him and welcome him into relationship, and after a brief stint of him living with me (Brandon), we were able to help him move into his first apartment. We had a housewarming party for him and decked out the place. Seeing the sense of pride glow on his face was something we'll never forget. Over the years that Luis was with us, he came to know Jesus, was baptized surrounded by hundreds of people cheering for him, and became an integral part of our church family.

Allow the gospel to transform you so that you can become intentional about welcoming with the warmth of Christ those from abroad. Go out of your way to initiate relationship with those who look like they may be new to the culture without making them feel weird. Don't let their experience here, however brief or long, not include a hospitable Christian with an open life and home. The world has come to us, so let's open our doors and watch God bring about change.[4]

QUESTIONS TO CONSIDER

- Which types of people mentioned in this chapter are currently in your life? In what ways can you take an active step to show them biblical hospitality?
- What feelings do these big steps of biblical hospitality bring to mind? Do you find yourself overwhelmed with the thought of having someone in your home long-term or even adopting a child? What objections do you have? What truths do you need to remember to counter these objections?
- What changes has God brought into your life as you've read this book? How can you continue to take steps forward?

CHAPTER 12

FINALLY HOME

The world changes through the ordinary actions of God's people. Do a simple Google search for "change the world." Among the 1.1 billion search results, you will find all sorts of exciting and significant projects—dig a well in Africa, adopt children from local orphanages, start a business, or get an advanced degree. These may all be worthwhile suggestions, but they can leave us feeling overwhelmed and helpless.

How am I supposed to do something like that? we think. *I can't even make it through Tuesday without spilling coffee in my lap.*

So we conclude that the best thing for us is leave all of that world-changing stuff to someone else, someone with a high capacity, more money, or added margin in life. We will just settle for our mundane, uneventful, average existence.

What we've argued throughout this book is that the simplest way to change the world is to leverage your ordinary life for His history-sweeping mission of hospitality.

In chapter 3 we covered the truth that all of human history is a story of God's hospitality to those who have rebelled against Him. God made a home for humans in the garden of Eden, and ever since our first parents sinned and were barred from that garden, God has been working to reconcile people from every nation to Himself and make a home where we can dwell with Him again—this time, forever.

There is a day coming when something truly significant will happen—something that will culminate God's plan throughout all human history. The ordinary, seemingly insignificant details of our lives are all moving forward to this one, final day. Revelation 19:6–9 gives one picture of what this final reconciliation, this eternal home-coming of sorts, will look like:

> I heard what seemed to be the voice of a great multitude, like the roar of many waters and like the sound of mighty peals of thunder, crying out, "Hallelujah! For the Lord our God the Almighty reigns. Let us rejoice and exult and give him the glory, for the marriage of the Lamb has come, and his Bride has made herself ready; it was granted her to clothe herself with fine linen, bright and pure"—for the fine linen is the righteous deeds of the saints. And the angel said to me, "Write this: Blessed are those who are invited to the marriage supper of the Lamb."

As Christians it's hard to read these prophetic words without a stir of emotion, as though some buried string in our soul is plucked and vibrates with sheer longing. We are going home! The swell we feel in our gut when we read of God's eternal banquet table is not some childish fantasy story, but our *destiny*. Our voices will be raised in that great multitude, like the roar of many waters and the sound of mighty thunder, with believers in Christ from throughout history.

We will sit at the table we were originally created for—the one where our Creator sits. We will no longer feast on "that which is not bread" (Isa. 55:2), but fill our heavenly bodies with the fare of heaven. All our desires will be met completely, like a cup running over, and all effects of sin and death and evil will be done away with for good (Rev. 21:1–5). All of the shadows of home we experienced on earth will give way to the realities, and we will be fully, finally, forever, home.

This is the joy set before us—an eternity with the hospitable God, enjoying relationship with Him and our many brothers and sisters around His table. Paul told us in 1 Corinthians 2:9 that however good we *think* it is going to be, that doesn't even compare to the reality of how good it *will* be: "As it is written, 'What no eye has seen, nor ear heard, nor the heart of man imagined, what God has prepared for those who love him.'"

But friend, as good as our eternal home is going to be, we are not there yet. We look forward to it with the utmost anticipation, while knowing that if the marriage supper of the Lamb hasn't yet happened, that means there is still work for us to do. There are people still to be invited to that eternal table, and God is patient with His plan, "not wishing that any should perish" apart from Him (2 Peter 3:9).

Such is our call as those who have been adopted into God's family: to keep spreading the good news that God is not distant or loveless or disinterested but gracious and slow to anger and actively working to be hospitable to us for all eternity.

> Let's mimic our hospitable God by welcoming others, as Christ has welcomed us.

In light of this reality, let's take seriously our call to model His gracious hospitality to our neighbors. Let's live in view of this eternal banquet table, and pray for our friends, coworkers, and anyone we come in contact with. Let's use our homes to be micro representations of that final banquet table—places where believers gather around the food and drink God has graciously provided, celebrating that God has brought us to Himself and opened that sacred space to all who are far from Him. Let's become relentlessly warm and welcoming because we've been relentlessly welcomed in Christ.

Imagine if your church embraced the call to model God's hospitality, both within the church and to those who don't yet know Jesus. Think what could be if your small group intentionally sought to welcome others into the community you have with one another, to let them see the gospel lived out in your relationships. What if Christians in your neighborhood banded together to own your street or building, seeking to advance the gospel one address at a time?

Turning our ordinary homes into weapons for the gospel and opening our normal lives to welcome others as Christ welcomed us is a calling that every single one of us can do. No Christian is above or below this call to practice biblical hospitality as a way of life, and no other practice so clearly and simply puts the welcoming grace of our God on display.

So Christian, let's do this, and let's do it together. Let's mimic our hospitable God by welcoming others, as Christ has welcomed us, into our lives and our homes, all the while praying they will be with us when we are finally home.

Doing so might just be the simplest way to change the world.

SIX-WEEK SMALL GROUP GUIDE

HOW TO USE THIS GUIDE

The goal of *The Simplest Way to Change the World* is not necessarily to get you into a group, but to help you walk with others as you seek to make hospitality a way of life. However, groups do tend to be a great framework for community and application to take place. It only makes sense to discuss and process these ideas with other people with whom you are doing life.

The hope is for missional communities, small groups, Sunday school classes, church-plant core teams, church staffs, and even entire churches to work through the book together and allow it to shape the way they leverage their homes and lives for the sake of the gospel.

This study guide is intended to be a supportive resource for any leader or group facilitator. We have provided a "Tips for Leading" resource and then a simple, straightforward guide for the six-week study.

TIPS FOR LEADING THIS SMALL GROUP

1. Journal through the assigned reading. Consult commentaries, such as the Bible in Easy English (www.easyenglish.info), to add insight to the original meaning and context of the passages.

2. Pray. Answer all the questions from each week as part of your prep work. Then pray that God will awaken ideas for how each person in the group can make hospitality a way of life.

3. Leave room for other voices. The first level of group conversation is you talking to the group. The next level is that the group talks back to you. The third level is the group talks to each other. When God talks to people, the group is functioning on the highest and healthiest level.

You talk > We talk back > We talk to each other > God talks to us

4. Start your formal group time by connecting. Be creative and have fun. Give the group something easy to talk about before moving into "Heart Matters."

5. Watch the clock. Because of the open-ended approach to the questions, the deeper the conversations the greater the time challenge.

- Clearly identify your end time at the beginning of the formal meeting.

- Let people answer questions one-on-one and in triads.

- Decide in advance how much time you will spend on each section.

- Designate a group timekeeper.

- Keep moving. Conclude the meeting before people become aware of the clock.

6. Review the past week's debrief. Coach your group toward action. Reviewing next steps from the last gathering raises accountability for hearing God and following through. Have participants pray for each other concerning their next steps.

7. Become a great listener. Listen to what God says to you about others. Listen beyond what is normal and comfortable for you.

8. Be creative. Anything can get boring, even highly engaging approaches to group learning. If you are not creative, find someone in your group who is and let that person help you.

SMALL GROUP STUDY
WEEK 1

BEFORE THE GROUP GATHERS, HAVE EVERYONE READ:
- *The Simplest Way to Change the World*, chapters 1 and 2
- Romans 12:1–2

HEART MATTERS
- How do you view your home? Are you more prone to view it as a place of retreat or as a weapon for the gospel? Why?
- Why do most of us assume that ordinary steps of obedience are insignificant? What biblical evidence do we have that this is not true?
- What assumptions about hospitality did you bring with you as you began this study?

SOUND BITES
"Many Christians have bought into the cultural view that our homes are our personal and private fortresses. In our combined twenty-plus years of pastoring, we have observed that the way a typical Christian thinks about their home isn't all that different from how a typical non-Christian thinks: *It's the place I eat, sleep, relax, and entertain myself—by myself*" (p. 18).

"When it comes to pursuing biblical hospitality as a way of life, we immediately happen upon a major obstacle: almost everything in our culture is set up to hinder us from pursuing it. Much like those two young fish, we are so pulled by the drudgery of our everyday lives that we fail to stay attuned to God's call on us to be missional. Our default is to swim along with the current of our culture, not giving a single thought about the water that surrounds our every move and pushes us in the opposite direction of intentional mission" (p. 29).

ZOOM IN

Read Romans 12:1–2.

- How does Paul say a Christian should relate to the pattern of this world?
- Why does the mission of a Christian's life necessitate counter-cultural living? What happens if you consistently follow the world's values rather than God's values?
- How is hospitality a countercultural practice?
- Which verse did God want you to see/hear/apply?

DEBRIEF

- Which of the four cultural currents (isolation, retreat, entertainment, busyness) that work against hospitality hinder you from using your home as a weapon for the gospel?
- What changes would you need to make for hospitality to become a way of life for you?

SMALL GROUP STUDY
WEEK 2

BEFORE THE GROUP GATHERS, HAVE EVERYONE READ:
- *The Simplest Way to Change the World*, chapters 3 and 4
- 2 Corinthians 5:17–21

HEART MATTERS
- Is "hospitable" a virtue you typically use to speak about God? Why is the work of Jesus a demonstration of God's hospitality?
- When Christians practice hospitality they are modeling the heart of God. How does this serve as the primary motivation for hospitality?
- How has your relationship with God been influenced by the care and hospitality of others? What impacted you most about the love of others?

SOUND BITES
"Throughout the saga of history, God consistently initiates relationship. He is a gracious host, constantly welcoming in wayward sinners who deserve His wrath—a people whose only hope is that He would show them undeserved hospitality" (p. 41).

"After all, a hospitable God will create a hospitable people to represent Him in every age throughout history" (p. 45).

ZOOM IN
Read 2 Corinthians 5:17–21.
- What does it mean to be reconciled to God? How is this a picture of God's hospitality?
- What is the mission of a Christian, based on this passage? How should this mission shape your life?
- What does your current lifestyle communicate about God's

character? If you are a Christian, imagine yourself as a walking billboard for the gospel. What are you saying to the world?

DEBRIEF

- How have your experiences with the church shaped how you view its people? Are you more apt to think of the church as a place of love and hospitality or a place of judgment and disunity?
- In a time when the church is increasingly marginalized and known for negative stereotypes, how can a return to biblical hospitality change its reputation?

SMALL GROUP STUDY
WEEK 3

BEFORE THE GROUP GATHERS, HAVE EVERYONE READ:
- *The Simplest Way to Change the World*, chapters 5 and 6
- Acts 2:42–47; 4:32–37

HEART MATTERS
- What evidence do you see that your friends are longing for relationships with others? How does this longing present an incredible opportunity for you to practice biblical hospitality?
- Why is it easier to disagree with others from a distance or behind a keyboard than it is to love our actual neighbors? How might genuine, Christlike love provide a context in which you might have more meaningful conversations?
- In what ways is God calling you to ask, "What if?" How is God drawing your heart to invest in particular people or places?

SOUND BITES
"When we are included, invited, cared for, recognized, and enfolded into the warmth of relationship, something in our psyches knows that this is the type of connection we were designed for. This inner knowledge reflects the statement God made over Adam in Genesis 2:18, that it is not good for man to be alone" (p. 56).

"While hospitality has always been a primary way God has advanced His mission, our culture in particular presents a remarkable context for practicing it to go viral. People who are far from Jesus need to be recognized, included, and invited into village-like relationships" (p. 57).

ZOOM IN
Read Acts 2:42–47; 4:32–37.

- What descriptions of hospitality do you observe in the life of the first church?
- How do you observe these same marks in the life of the church to which you belong?
- How are you personally working to foster these marks in the church?

DEBRIEF

- What one step toward practicing hospitality have you taken since you began reading this book? How did it go? What observations did you make about the importance of hospitality?
- What happens if hospitality is not accompanied by "our lives as well"? Why is it essential that we open our homes and our lives to others?
- How does your view of your home change if you see it as a hospital designed for care and healing?

SMALL GROUP STUDY
WEEK 4

BEFORE THE GROUP GATHERS, HAVE EVERYONE READ:
- *The Simplest Way to Change the World*, chapters 7 and 8
- Ephesians 2

HEART MATTERS
- What excuses do you make in order to avoid practicing biblical hospitality? What truths do you need to remember in order to counter these objections?
- Who can you team up with in order to begin practicing a lifestyle of hospitality? Obviously, if you are married, this is the place to begin. But what other neighbors or church members could you partner with as well? How could this make this practice easier?
- Did you implement any of the practical steps outlined in the chapters you read this week? If so, how did these help you practice a hospitable lifestyle? What other steps could you take to build "hospitality reminders" into your life?

SOUND BITES
"The first thing to remember on this journey is the nature of God. He is sovereign, meaning He rules over all things. He orchestrates all things for His purposes, including who lives, works, and plays near you. You may not consider these people as gifts from God because they have been part of your life for so long that they've become a backdrop. You are prone to miss them. But every day you pass people who could be blessed through your hospitality" (p. 93).

"Meeting your neighbors may not always be easy, but it is possible! Once you get into the habit of identifying those you can invite into your world, you can move on to building rhythms for making hospitality a way of life" (p. 101).

ZOOM IN

Read Ephesians 2.
- What all did God do for sinful humans, based on this chapter?
- What did God do to bring about the unity of His people? How does practicing biblical hospitality foster this unity?
- What steps can you take to demonstrate that all people—regardless of color, financial background, or political leanings—are worthy of love and respect? How can you demonstrate this through opening your home?

DEBRIEF

- What steps could you take to initiate a conversation with someone new this week?
- What is one creative step you could take to practice biblical hospitality? What would you need to do in order to make this creative idea a reality?

SMALL GROUP STUDY
WEEK 5

BEFORE THE GROUP GATHERS, HAVE EVERYONE READ:
- *The Simplest Way to Change the World*, chapters 9 and 10
- 1 John 4:7–21

HEART MATTERS
- Which of the weekly, monthly, or yearly rhythms presented in chapter 9 is most appealing to you? Which ones do you think would work best in the places where you live, work, and play?
- What normal events could you turn into a means of practicing hospitality? Which event is the next one on the calendar— maybe a kid's birthday party or a holiday? What can you do to infuse this event with purpose and mission?

SOUND BITES
"Since we seek to be hospitable people, and not merely people who practice hospitality, we need to find ways to build our lives around this goal. Sure, it will take time. But with a little thought and practice, those rhythms will become habits, and habits become a way of life" (p. 103–4).

"Our mission, as ambassadors of Christ, is to share the good news of Jesus' work through His life, death, burial, and resurrection. This is the true hope for the world. As a result, we can't keep from speaking the gospel to those we love—or at least we should not be able to" (p. 119).

ZOOM IN
Read 1 John 4:7–21.
- What do you observe about God from this passage? How should God's character be reflected in the lives of His people?

- How should your salvation motivate you to live a hospitable life?
- How can the love of Christians for other Christians allow outsiders to catch a glimpse of the gospel? How might these same relationships cause you to neglect showing hospitality to those who are far from God?
- What steps can you take to open your community with Christians to those who are far from God?

DEBRIEF

- Which of the practical tips for moving a conversation to the gospel comes most naturally for you? Which of these tips is most challenging? What steps could you take to grow in these weaker areas?
- How does your view of mission and hospitality change with the knowledge that God goes before you, lives inside you, and accomplishes the work for you? How should these truths encourage and motivate you?

SMALL GROUP STUDY
WEEK 6

BEFORE THE GROUP GATHERS, HAVE EVERYONE READ:
- *The Simplest Way to Change the World*, chapters 11 and 12
- Revelation 21

HEART MATTERS
- Which types of people mentioned in chapter 11 are currently in your life? How can you take an active step to show them biblical hospitality?
- What feelings do these big steps of biblical hospitality bring to mind? Do you find yourself overwhelmed with the thought of having someone in your home long-term or even adopting a child? What are your objections? What truths do you need to remember in order to counter these objections?

SOUND BITES
"There is a great need for orphan care around the world and also in our own backyards. Christians should lead the charge to be diligently hospitable to children in need. This is a beautiful and compelling act of hospitality that puts God's lavish hospitality to us on full display" (p. 138).

"Turning our ordinary homes into weapons for the gospel and opening our normal lives to welcome others as Christ welcomed us is a calling that every single one of us can do. No Christian is above or below this call to practice biblical hospitality as a way of life, and no other practice so clearly and simply puts the welcoming grace of our God on display" (p. 145).

ZOOM IN

Read Revelation 21.
- How is all of human history going to end?
- In what ways does this truth motivate you to live on mission today?
- How are the pictures John paints in this chapter a portrait of God's hospitality?

DEBRIEF

- What changes has God brought into your life as a result of this study?
- How can you continue to take steps forward now that you are finished reading?
- In what ways can you encourage other members of your church or small group to embrace the mission of biblical hospitality?

RESOURCES FOR MORE HOSPITALITY ENCOURAGEMENT

We do not consider ourselves to have cornered the market on the subject of hospitality. There are a number of works that have committed sections or specific chapters to this biblical practice, and mining them for additional guidance can be helpful. Few books spend their entirety discussing Christian hospitality, which was part of our drive to write *The Simplest Way to Change the World*. Below we recommend resources that have been helpful to us and to our friends in the journey toward living out biblical hospitality.

Making Room by Christine D. Pohl (She offers great insight into the history of Christian hospitality.)

Everyday Church by Tim Chester and Steve Timmis, specifically chapter 4

A Meal with Jesus by Tim Chester, chapter 4

Saturate by Jeff Vanderstelt, part 5

Next Door as It Is in Heaven by Lance Ford and Brad Brisco, chapter 6

Building Friendships by Dave Arnold, chapter 6

Staying Is the New Going by Alan Briggs, chapter 8

The Divine Commodity by Skye Jethani, chapter 8

Life in Community by Dustin Willis, chapter 11 (We are admittedly biased on this one.)

The Art of Neighboring by Jay Pathak and Dave Runyon

NOTES

Chapter 1: Small Things Can Change the World

1. In Matthew 28:18–20, Jesus gave us directions on how to live, which has become known as the Great Commission: "All authority in heaven and on earth has been given to me. Go therefore and make disciples of all nations, baptizing them in the name of the Father and of the Son and of the Holy Spirit, teaching them to observe all that I have commanded you. And behold, I am with you always, to the end of the age."

2. "The Daisy Cutter Doctrine," SkyeJethani.com, February 25, 2016, http://skyejethani.com/the-daisy-cutter-doctrine-2/.

3. Ibid.

Chapter 2: We Know What You Are Thinking . . .

1. David Foster Wallace, transcription of the 2005 Kenyon Commencement Address, May 21, 2005, https://web.ics.purdue.edu/~drkelly/DFWKenyon Address2005.pdf.

2. For the record, we are in no way hating on HGTV. In fact, we love it. It's wonderful to see different homes, watch how people make decisions, and grow insanely jealous over the ways the most talented people remodel lame houses. It's especially fun to watch during those seasons when you are moving and you can get ideas you probably won't have the money or talent to implement.

3. Jenna Goudreau, "So Begins a Quiet Revolution of the 50 Percent," Forbes .com, January 30, 2012, http://www.forbes.com/sites/jennagoudreau/2012/01/30/quiet-revolution-of-the-50-percent-introverts-susan-cain/#31fc9adc 6ba5.

4. To be exact, four hours and thirty-one minutes of live television, plus thirty-three minutes of DVR/time-shifted TV. "The Total Audience Report, Q1 2016," The Nielsen Company, June 27, 2016, http://www.nielsen.com/us/en/insights/reports/2016/the-total-audience-report-q1-2016.html.

5. To be exact, one hour and thirty-nine minutes on smartphone apps and thirty-one minutes on tablet apps. Ibid.

6. http://www.urbandictionary.com/define.php?term=show%20hole.

Chapter 3: The Hospitable God

1. "I will put enmity between you and the woman, and between your offspring and her offspring; he shall bruise your head, and you shall bruise his heel" (Gen. 3:15).

2. "We are ambassadors for Christ, God making his appeal through us. We implore you on behalf of Christ, be reconciled to God" (2 Cor. 5:20).

Chapter 4: A Hospitable People

1. "I will bless those who bless you, and him who dishonors you I will curse, and in you all the families of the earth shall be blessed" (Gen. 12:3).

2. Quoted in "Praying for Enemies," Skye Jethani, With God Daily Devotional, https://skyejethani.com/devotionals/2016/06/19/praying-for-enemies-3/.

3. Rodney Stark, *The Rise of Christianity* (Princeton, NJ: Princeton University Press, 1996), 82.

4. This concept of hospitality as recognition of people made in God's image comes from and is explored more thoroughly in *Making Room: Recovering Hospitality as a Christian Tradition* by Christine Pohl.

Chapter 5: A Timely Opportunity

1. Bunmi Laditan, "I Miss the Village," The Huffington Post, July 22, 2014, http://www.huffingtonpost.com/bunmi-laditan/i-miss-the-village_b_5585677.html.

2. Christine Pohl, *Making Room: Recovering Hospitality as a Christian Tradition* (Grand Rapids, MI: Wm. B. Eerdmans, 1999), 64.

3. Emily Adler, "Social Media Engagement: The Surprising Facts About How Much Time People Spend on the Major Social Networks," *Business Insider*, July 7, 2016, http://www.businessinsider.com/social-media-engagement-statistics-2013-12.

4. Skye Jethani, *The Divine Commodity* (Grand Rapids, MI: Zondervan, 2009), 145.

5. Maureen O'Connor, "Addicted to Likes: How Social Media Feeds Our Neediness," *New York* magazine, February 20, 2014, http://nymag.com/thecut/2014/02/addicted-to-likes-social-media-makes-us-needier.html.

6. Shalini Misra, "The iPhone Effect," Virginia Tech School of Public and International Affairs, http://eab.sagepub.com/content/48/2/275.abstract.

7. "The Most Post-Christian Cities," Barna:Cities, http://cities.barna.org/the-most-post-christian-cities-in-america/.

8. "Speaking the truth in love, we are to grow up in every way into him who is the head, into Christ" (Eph. 4:15).

9. Rosaria Butterfield, "My Train Wreck Conversion," *Christianity Today*, February 7, 2013, http://www.christianitytoday.com/ct/2013/january-february/my-train-wreck-conversion.html.

10. Ibid.

Chapter 6: The End Goal of Hospital(ity)

1. http://stuffchristianslike.net/2010/11/16/the-jesus-juke/.

2. John Piper, "Strategic Hospitality," *Desiring God*, August 25, 1985, http://www.desiringgod.org/messages/strategic-hospitality.

Chapter 7: Setting Yourself Up for Success

1. As Paul said: "In all things I have shown you that by working hard in this way we must help the weak and remember the words of the Lord Jesus, how he himself said, 'It is more blessed to give than to receive'" (Acts 20:35).

Chapter 8: How Do You Meet Your Neighbors?

1. By practicing the Always Rule, I'm trying to live what 2 Timothy 1:7 says: "God has not given us a spirit of timidity, but of power and love and discipline" (NASB).

2. Clint Clifton, July 16, 2016, https://twitter.com/clintjclifton.

3. http://www.meetup.com.

Chapter 9: Practical Rhythms of Hospitality

1. "The Fundamental Command: Love One Another," https://www.biblegateway.com/resources/commentaries/IVP-NT/1JohFundamental-Command-Love-One.

Chapter 10: How Do You Get to the Gospel?

1. For example: "Contribute to the needs of the saints and seek to show hospitality" (Rom. 12:13) and "Having a reputation for good works: if she has brought up children, has shown hospitality, has washed the feet of the saints, has cared for the afflicted, and has devoted herself to every good work" (1 Tim. 5:10).

2. Charles H. Spurgeon, "A Sermon and a Reminiscence," *Sword and the Trowel,* March 1873, http://www.spurgeon.org/s_and_t/srmn1873.php.

3. If you would like a tool that helps you to prepare a presentation, we recommend *3 Circles: Life Conversation Guide,* http://lifeonmissionbook.com/conversation-guide.

4. David Platt, *Radical: Taking Back Your Faith from the American Dream* (Colorado Springs: Multnomah Books, 2010), 87–88.

5. If you want to grow more in gospel fluency, we recommend checking out Jeff Vanderstelt's articles and sermons on the topic at http://wearesoma.com/resources/watch/gospel-fluency/.

6. "If I speak in the tongues of men and of angels, but have not love, I am a noisy gong or a clanging cymbal" (1 Cor. 13:1).

7. Consider the Israelites who struggled under slavery: "During those many days the king of Egypt died, and the people of Israel groaned because of their slavery and cried out for help. Their cry for rescue from slavery came up to God. And God heard their groaning, and God remembered his covenant with Abraham, with Isaac, and with Jacob. God saw the people of Israel—and God knew" (Ex. 2:23–25).

8. http://www.russellmoore.com/books/onward/.

9. "He will wipe away every tear from their eyes, and death shall be no more, neither shall there be mourning, nor crying, nor pain anymore, for the former things have passed away" (Rev. 21:4).

Chapter 11: Other Ways to Leverage Your Home for Mission

1. https://www.biblegateway.com/resources/commentaries/IVP-NT/Jas/
   Practice-Pure-Religion.

2. AdoptUSKids reports that there are more than 400,000 US children in foster
   care. http://www.adoptuskids.org/meet-the-children/children-in-foster-care/
   about-the-children. In 2015, Georgia had 11,551 children in state custody,
   reported by the Georgia Division of Family & Children Services: http://dfcs
   .dhs.georgia.gov/sites/dfcs.dhs.georgia.gov/files/Adoptions%20Page%20-%20
   2016.pdf.

3. Ephesians 2:11–13: "Remember that at one time you Gentiles in the flesh,
   called 'the uncircumcision' by what is called the circumcision, which is made
   in the flesh by hands—remember that you were at that time separated from
   Christ, alienated from the commonwealth of Israel and strangers to the covenants of promise, having no hope and without God in the world. But now in
   Christ Jesus you who once were far off have been brought near by the blood of
   Christ."

4. For additional information on this topic, we recommend *Seeking Refuge: On
   the Shores of the Global Refugee Crisis* by Issam Smeir, Matthew Soerens, and
   Stephan Bauman, and *Welcoming the Stranger: Justice, Compassion & Truth in
   the Immigration Debate* by Jenny Hwang Yang and Matthew Soerens.

ACKNOWLEDGMENTS

From Dustin:

Leveraging our home for mission has been some of the most fun we've ever had. Before making a significant shift toward hospitality, my wife and I didn't have a neighbor we could genuinely call a friend. Now having lived with the intentional pursuit of hospitality since our move to Atlanta, we have developed lifelong friendships with neighbors who are now like family. It's incredible to watch God take something like our homes, which we used to view in self-serving ways, and turn them into a vital part of how He's reaching those around us. Thank you, Chadbourne of Alpharetta, for giving us the opportunity to make hospitality a way of life.

Renie—You lead the way for what it looks like to live out hospitality. Thank you for setting the rhythms in our home, for welcoming people in, for displaying grace, and for speaking into the lives of those who cross the threshold of our door. I love you and I look forward to seeing the story that God writes for our household.

Jack and Piper—You guys have been so encouraging throughout this writing process, especially in what has been an extremely busy season of change. You continually tell me to "hurry up and write" and those words many times pushed me to keep going. Your *our lives as well* attitude is incredible, and I believe that God will use both of you and your future homes to help change the world. I love you.

Brandon Clements—Beginning to end, you made this book happen. To partner with you on this project has been incredible. Thank you not only for inking so much of the content, but for leading the church to live out these words through the example you and Kristi set. You were the first intern I ever "hired." Thanks for working for free. Doing ministry with you has been a complete blessing.

My Family—Ma, Pa, Mandy, Wendy, Joey, Michael—I am grateful for how you each advance the gospel through using your home(s). You consistently display and speak grace into people's lives around your own tables. Maddie—As you are now in college, I already see hospitality becoming a way of life for you and I pray God uses it to change your campus. Will, Ben, Gracie, and Janie—I pray that you will follow the example your parents have set and that you will be revolutionary in pursuing Jesus' mission. Frank, Cindy, Merritt, Jeff, and Kate—Thank you for the hospitality that you have shown me since day one.

My Atlanta Family—To seek to name everyone would be a book in itself, as so many have shaped this book's vision. Our neighbors who make up Chadbourne—We are privileged to call you neighbors. To those who make up Fairwind Court—There is nothing like doing life alongside you. Micah Millican, Andrew Kistler, Vince Barron, Lee Cunningham, Shane Critser, Alex Melber—Doing life in ATL with you guys is a daily encouragement in my journey to be like Jesus.

My NAMB Family—Kevin Ezell, Carlos Ferrer, Kim Robinson, and the board of trustees—Thank you for the opportunity to be part of the incredible vision to see *every church on mission* and for allowing me to pursue my personal passion of writing. To the teams I am privileged to serve with—I am grateful for you and the heart you have for the church.

Ginger Kolbaba—Three books in the last twenty-three months. This feat would have been absolutely impossible without having you as the primary editor on all three. Grateful for your God-given ability to find the best words and the humor to make it fun along the way.

Matt Rogers—Your gift for crafting words is mind-blowing. Thank you for being a great friend along this journey and for jumping in when we needed your wisdom. Grateful for you and the gifts God has given you.

Kent Bateman, Landon and Jordan Thompson—Truly grateful for your creativity and the design of the front cover that represents the heart behind this work. I love the fact that this book represents hearts like yours. We love you guys!

The Team at Moody—Thank you for the opportunity to partner with you guys on what is now book three. It has been an incredible journey over the last two years. Duane Sherman—Thank you for your partnership and the example that you set in the way of hospitality.

From Brandon:

Kristi Clements—Thanks for always supporting my passion of writing, and for being my biggest source of encouragement for more than a decade. Thanks for always being up for leveraging our home for the gospel and for training our kids that the God we serve is an inviting, welcoming, and gracious God. I know this book was written in a season that was very busy and tiring for you, so thanks for your grace, patience, and sacrifice for the time this project took me away from you and our crazy, wonderful kids.

Sully, Isla, and Jeremiah—You kids don't even know what the word *hospitality* means yet, but you are always up for making new friends and welcoming them into our home. I pray for you, I adore you all, and I can't wait to see what God does through your lives. I am immeasurably grateful that I get to be your dad.

My Midtown Family—Man, it's been such a fun ride. Over the last ten years I've learned what a healthy church is supposed to look like, been humbled by the staggering grace Jesus shows through you all, and been inspired countless times by ordinary believers leveraging their ordinary lives to join in God's mission to save the planet. By His grace we have become what we've always been after: a "Jesus-centered family on mission with Him," and I've never seen anything more beautiful. Thanks for helping teach me that a hospitable God creates a hospitable people, and for having open homes and open lives for the sake of the gospel.

My LifeGroup—Thanks for gathering in our home every Thursday night to talk about Jesus, confess our sins to one another, and pray for one another. Thanks for seeking to practice hospitality in your neighborhoods, jobs, and hobbies, and for always warmly accepting new people no matter how large we grow. It is an honor to raise our kids together, be church family, and live on mission with you.

Dustin Willis—Thanks for taking a chance on a brash college student who walked up to you and said, "Can I move to Columbia and intern with you?" It's been a blast to work with you again. I am incredibly grateful for your friendship and the way God has used you in my life.

Mema—I first saw hospitality lived out through your example of welcoming anyone and everyone into your home. Your house was always such a bright spot of warmth and grace, and it's no wonder kids and people of all ages have always wanted to gather at the brick house up on the hill. Your home is one of my favorite places because you model making other people feel at home there. Thanks for your example and love for Jesus. I love you and am beyond thankful for you.

Foreword by DAVID PLATT

LIFE
ON MISSION

Joining the Everyday Mission of God

DUSTIN WILLIS | AARON COE

WITH THE SEND NETWORK TEAM

MOODY
Publishers™

From the Word to Life

+RƎ⊃I⊂ꓥL

WITH DAVID PLATT

Radical with David Platt, a half-hour national teaching program, airs daily on Moody Radio. Bestselling author, sought-after conference speaker, and pastor, David Platt brings to each program solid, passionate Bible teaching aimed at equipping and mobilizing Christians to make disciples among the nations so that the Lord receives the glory due His name.

www.radicalwithdavidplatt.org